12 LAMPARD!

BIG INTERVIEWS!

RONALDO! **18**

KU-560-540

14 ENGLAND TEAMTALK!

4 PLANET FOOTY FRENZY!

COOL names in footy!

BRUCE ARENA
USA

I'M THE BOSS OF THIS ARENA, DUDES!

Mmmm, that's a snack for later!

BOGEYS

France star Zinedine Zidane fishes out a big bogey! Yu

Deutschland
England
Olympiastadion München
1 : 5
01. SEP. 2001

1 GEARED UP FOR GERMANY!
The last time England played in Germany we did 'em 5-1 with a hat-trick from Li'l MO! Germany must be our lucky country!

Germany 2006... this can be the year that England win the World Cup again! Beckham thinks we can win, Rooney thinks we can win it and here are five more reasons why the World Cup can have England's name on it!

COME ON!

WE CAN WIN!

3 BECKS IS BACK!
David Beckham wasn't in top form at Euro 2004, but now the England captain is back to his best! Result!

4 FANTASTIC FANS!
Not many fans could get to the last World Cup in Asia, but this time England will have huge support in Germany!

THREE LIONS ON A SHIRT!

Oi!

STOP CHUCKING BOG ROLL AT ME!

WOW, I REALLY NEED A HAIRCUT!

ARM WRESTLE, JT?

I'LL BEAT YOU, RIO!

FERDINAND 5

6

2 ROCK-SOLID DEFENCE!

Terry, Ferdinand, Cole, Neville, King – England have got the best defenders in the world! JT and the lads will stop 'em all!

IT!

ALL THE WAY TO THE FINAL, MATCH!

WHO WILL SCORE FIRST?

England are gonna score tons of goals in the World Cup, but which player will score first?

Wayne Rooney		✓
David Beckham		✓
Michael Owen		✓
Frank Lampard		✓
Steven Gerrard		✓
John Terry		✓
Jermain Defoe		✓

5 ROONEY ROCKS!

Wayne is the key to England winning the World Cup. So if the striker can stay fit, the World Cup is as good as ours!

WORLD CUP WRESTLING!

Seconds out, round one! Check out top footy stars working on some wrestling mega moves!

HOLLAND

DON'T CALL ME AN OLD MAN AGAIN!

Edwin van der Sar grabs Dirk Kuyt in a nasty headlock jam!

ARRGGHH!

YER STUCK! HA, HA!

BRAZIL

Robinho tries his best body-slam out on his mate Julio Baptista!

The England squad practise their gut-barge moves! Bosh!

GET IN MY BELLY!

ENGLAND

WORLD CUP SAFETY!

Ruud, Figo and Adriano look left, then right and left again before walking on to the pitch!

This safety stuff is easy!

RACE FOR THE GOLDEN BOOT!

World Cup 2006 will be packed with super strikers, but who will be the tournament's top scorer and win the Golden Boot trophy?

WAZZA WANTS THE TROPHY!

IF I DON'T SCORE, I'M GONNA SCREAM!

LUCA TONI
ITALY

CLUB: Fiorentina **AGE:** 28
TOP SKILL: The powerful striker is fantastic in the air!
Luca Toni bagged loads of goals in Serie A last season! If he can score early on, then he may be a real Golden Boot contender!

GOLDEN BOOT RATING

WAYNE ROONEY
ENGLAND

CLUB: Man. United **AGE:** 20
TOP SKILL: Running at the opposition defenders with pace!
He's one of the hottest players on the planet! If Wayne racks up the goals in the group stage, he'll want to scoop this top award!

GOLDEN BOOT RATING

RUUD VAN NISTELROOY
HOLLAND

CLUB: Man. United **AGE:** 29
TOP SKILL: He's always in the right place at the right time!
Ruud's a top striker and Holland will hope to reach the semi-finals at least, so he should have plenty of chances to hit the net!

GOLDEN BOOT RATING

ANDRIY SHEVCHENKO
UKRAINE

CLUB: AC Milan **AGE:** 29
TOP SKILL: Lethal shooting from outside the box!
Ukraine may struggle to reach the knockout stages, so super striker Sheva needs to bag loads early on to win the Golden Boot!

GOLDEN BOOT RATING

Did you know it has been 40 years since England last won the World Cup? It's also been 16 years since England last made the WC semi-finals!

COOL names in footy!

JOSH WOLFF
USA

WATCH OUT, COZ THE WOLFF WILL BITE YA!

BIG RON'S READY TO WIN IT AGAIN!

RONALDO
BRAZIL

CLUB: Real Madrid **AGE:** 29
TOP SKILL: Turning defenders inside out with his quick feet!

Ronaldo has been banging in the goals for Real Madrid in 2006! The Brazilian is the fave to win another World Cup Golden Boot!

GOLDEN BOOT RATING

I'M HUNGRY FOR GOALS! YUM, YUM!

THIERRY HENRY
FRANCE

CLUB: Arsenal **AGE:** 28
TOP SKILL: Curling powerful shots past the 'keeper!

France had a rubbish World Cup in 2002, when Henry was sent off and didn't score a single goal! This time he's out for revenge!

GOLDEN BOOT RATING

COOL captains!

Check out these flashy stars who will be wearing the captain's armband in Germany!

DAVID BECKHAM
ENGLAND

MICHAEL BALLACK
GERMANY

CAFU
BRAZIL

FABIO CANNAVARO
ITALY

DIDIER DROGBA
IVORY COAST

ZINEDINE ZIDANE
FRANCE

LUIS FIGO
PORTUGAL

JUAN PABLO SORIN
ARGENTINA

MARK VIDUKA
AUSTRALIA

DWIGHT YORKE
TRINIDAD & TOBAGO

you is ugly!
Germany 'keeper Oliver Kahn is one very ugly momma!

WHAT BOOTS DOES...
Wayne Rooney wear?

Nike Air Zoom Total 90 III!

ENGLAND'S TOP SECRET BASE CAMP!
REVEALED

Beckham and his England mates have already sorted out their flash hotel and training camp for the trip to Germany – they're gonna stay at a luxury castle in the middle of the Black Forest! Check out MATCH's wicked guide to England's World Cup HQ!

MATCH can't wait for the World Cup to start – but how much do you actually know about the host country Germany? Here's our mini guide...

TOP GRUB!
MOST GERMAN PEOPLE LOVE TO EAT SAUSAGES AND PICKLED CABBAGE! YUK!

FOOTY GIANTS!
BAYERN MUNICH ARE GERMANY'S BIGGEST CLUB! THEY'VE WON FOUR EUROPEAN CUPS AND 19 BUNDESLIGA TITLES! WOAH!

THE HOTEL!
It's called the Schlosshotel Bühlerhöhe, and it costs up to £1,400 a NIGHT to stay there! It's got five floors and 90 rooms to stay in!

THE GOLF COURSE!
Li'l MO loves a game of golf and there are SIX courses for him to choose from!

I'm looking gut, baby!

SALON STYLE!
THE 'MULLET' HAIRSTYLE IS VERY POPULAR IN GERMANY, ERRRM... BUT NOT IN ENGLAND! HA, HA, HA!

THE TRAINING GROUND!
The lads will use FC Buhl's ground to train, perfect their tactics and practise celebrations!

THE POOL!
There's an indoor and outdoor swimming pool for the boys to splash about in! Cool!

DRESS FOR SUCCESS!
GERMANY'S NATIONAL DRESS IS CALLED 'LEDERHOSEN' MMMMM, FUNKY!

ROUGH GUIDE

PLANET FOOTY!

22!
That's how many games Mexico have lost in World Cup finals! It's a record!

SEND HIM OFF, REF!

MATCHY TRANSLATOR!
MATCHY makes sense of dodgy USA soccer speak!

WOAH, DUDE! THE UMPIRE'S GOTTA EJECT HIM FOR THAT TAKEDOWN!

WORLD CUP DEBUTS!

Seven countries will play in their first World Cup this summer! There are also loads of top footy stars who'll be making their debuts in the finals! Meet the best of the new boys...

ADRIANO
BRAZIL
Age: 24
Club: Inter Milan

The powerful Brazil striker was class in the Confederations Cup last year and will love playing at the World Cup too!

ENGLAND'S DEBUT BOYS!

These top England stars haven't played in a World Cup finals before!

WAYNE ROONEY
MAN. UNITED

STEVEN GERRARD
LIVERPOOL

FRANK LAMPARD
CHELSEA

JOHN TERRY
CHELSEA

PAUL ROBINSON
TOTTENHAM

DECO
PORTUGAL
Age: 28
Club: Barcelona

The playmaker has won the Champions League, UEFA Cup, La Liga and the Portuguese title! Now he's after World Cup glory!

ANDRIY SHEVCHENKO
UKRAINE
Age: 29
Club: AC Milan

Sheva has been one of Europe's deadliest strikers for years, and now he'll want to bang in the goals on the world stage!

XABI ALONSO
SPAIN
Age: 24
Club: Liverpool

Alonso's awesome passing has ripped up the Prem - now he's got the chance to show his talent to the whole world!

TAXI FOR THE ARGIES!

Argentina manager Jose Pekerman once quit footy to be a taxi driver before returning to the game!

TOURNAMENT HEROES!

Check out these crazy dudes who rocked World Cups!

PAOLO ROSSI!
ITALY
1982

DIEGO MARADONA!
ARGENTINA
1986

ROGER MILLA!
CAMEROON
1990

HRISTO STOICHKOV!
BULGARIA
1994

DAVOR SUKER!
CROATIA
1998

DEBUT TEAMS!

 ANGOLA

 GHANA

 IVORY COAST

SERBIA-MONTENEGRO

 TOGO

TRINIDAD & TOBAGO

UKRAINE

WHEN I WAS A LAD!

Brazil defender Cafu and France's wicked Zinedine Zidane are knocking on a bit now, but check out this pic from a few years back! Ha, ha!

WHO'S THIS FELLA?

YOU'LL SEE LOADS OF THIS BIG LION DURING THE SUMMER, COZ HE'S THE OFFICIAL WORLD CUP MASCOT! **MATCH** MEETS THE FURRY FELLA!

HEY MATCHY, FANCY A GAME?

GOLEO VI!

PILLE!

ER, WHO ARE THESE TWO OLD TIMERS?

IT'S PELE AND BECKENBAUER, YOU BIG DUMMY!

HEIDI KLUM!

BRING IT ON, FURRY BOY!

PILLE'S GOT MORE HAIR THAN YOU 'AVE, ZIZOU!

HEY, HOW YOU DOIN'?

FACTFILE!

Name: Goleo VI
Age: 18
Country: Germany
Best Mate: Pille the talking football!
Top skill: Roaring!

FRANK LAMPARD...
WE CAN BE HER

HOW EXCITED ARE YOU ABOUT YOUR WORLD CUP DEBUT?

"I'm really excited! I was on the verge of the squad for the 2002 World Cup but I didn't go, so that has made me even more hungry! Euro 2004 was a fantastic tournament, but the World Cup is even bigger and is the best competition you can play in. I'm more than excited about the summer!"

WHAT DO YOU MAKE OF ENGLAND'S GROUP, LAMPS?

"It's not the toughest, but it's not the easiest. Sweden have a very European style, Paraguay are always difficult to play and Trinidad & Tobago will be like a derby game, because we know some of their players in England!"

SO YOU'RE QUITE PLEASED WITH THE DRAW?

"Everyone can see that there are some groups that have stronger teams in them than other groups. Group C is a bit of a killer, but the countries that come through a really tough group like that will have lots of confidence for the knockout stages!"

WHICH TEAM WILL BE THE TOUGHEST TO BEAT?

"I think Sweden will be the toughest, because their record is good against us and they're a hard team to beat. They've got class, especially when you look at their forward players! I know more about Sweden than any of the other teams in our group, so I know that will be a tough game."

APART FROM ENGLAND, WHICH TEAMS CAN WIN IT?

"There are a few teams I could say here! If I had to pick one strong team then I would say Brazil. That's a fairly simple choice, because their whole squad is full of real top players. The big team from Europe may be Holland – they have some very good attacking flair in their team and they'll be really tough to play against!"

BUT ENGLAND HAVE SOME OF THE BEST PLAYERS!

"We've got fantastic players wherever you look! The defence is very strong and we've got back-up throughout the team if anybody's missing. Brazil have the flair players that everyone looks to, but we can match that with the squad we've got. If you look at our squad, there's no-one we should be scared of!"

OES!

Superstar midfielder **FRANK LAMPARD** tells **MATCH** why **ENGLAND** won't be scared of any team at the World Cup!

CAN ENGLAND GO ALL THE WAY?

"You have to say that we can go to the final. That's really the whole reason why we're going to Germany this summer! We're quite a confident bunch of players – we've got good individuals and a good team – so we'll go there happy and hoping to win the tournament. That's our aim!"

WHO WILL BE OUR KEY PLAYERS IN GERMANY?

"Wayne Rooney is a key player for us, because he links us up from back to front. He plays in a position that defenders find very difficult to mark, so he creates and finishes a lot of chances for us. It's very important to remember that the real key to England is our strength as a team, though!"

WHO WILL BE THE DARK HORSES OF THE TOURNAMENT?

"I watched quite a lot of the African Cup of Nations, and the Ivory Coast stood out as a team that won't be easy to deal with. When Didier Drogba saw the World Cup draw he knew it would be difficult, but he's a confident character and – if they get through their group – they could go far!"

ENGLAND...
MEET THE

Can **ENGLAND** win the World Cup for the first time since 1966? **MATCH** takes a look at Sven's stars who will be going for glory this summer!

GARY NEVILLE

Club: Man. United

Position: Right-back **Age:** 31

Debut: v Japan, 1995

There isn't a player in the England squad more experienced than Gaz Nev - this World Cup will be his fifth major tournament since breaking into the side before Euro '96! He's defo the team's first-choice right-back!

PAUL ROBINSON

Club: Tottenham

Position: Goalkeeper **Age:** 26

Debut: v Australia, 2003

As long as he doesn't get injured, Robbo will be England's No.1! He really deserves to be too, after a series of solid displays between the sticks. The Spurs 'keeper hardly ever makes a mistake either - he's rock-solid!

DAVID JAMES

Club: Man. City

Position: Goalkeeper **Age:** 35

Debut: v Mexico, 1997

Jamo's had a long England career and waited patiently for his big chance to be his country's first-choice 'keeper. Mistakes in the World Cup qualifier against Austria cost him his place, but he's great back-up for Robbo!

ASHLEY COLE

Club: Arsenal

Position: Left-back **Age:** 25

Debut: v Albania, 2001

Ash has made the left-back spot his own! He's brilliant going forward and his defensive skills have improved as well in recent years. His displays at Euro 2004 marked him out as one of the world's best - he'll be awesome!

SQUAD!

ENGLAND

JOHN TERRY

Club: Chelsea

Position: Centre-back **Age:** 25

Debut: v Serbia-Montenegro, 2003

JT's displays for club and country in the last two years have helped him become one of England's best central defenders! With his awesome power, strength in the air and leadership, Terry is a monster defender!

WAYNE BRIDGE

Club: Chelsea

Position: Left-back **Age:** 25

Debut: v Holland, 2002

Bridge battled back from a broken ankle last season and found it tough to get a game at Chelsea. But a loan move to Fulham gave him regular football, and now the ace attacking left-back is at his very best again!

SOL CAMPBELL

Club: Arsenal

Position: Centre-back **Age:** 31

Debut: v Hungary, 1996

Campbell picked up loads of injuries last season, which really affected his form, so he faces a battle to make the starting line-up! But he's got bags of experience and won't let England down if Sven calls on him!

JAMIE CARRAGHER

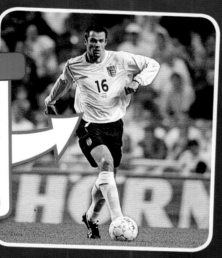

Club: Liverpool

Position: Centre-back **Age:** 28

Debut: v Hungary, 1999

If England didn't have so many quality centre-backs, Carragher would be a regular! The versatile Liverpool star is still a valuable squad member who can slot in anywhere across the back four and even in central midfield!

RIO FERDINAND

Club: Man. United

Position: Centre-back **Age:** 27

Debut: v Cameroon, 1997

The last 12 months have been a test for Rio, who was dropped by Sven for the World Cup qualifier against Austria at home. But he's back to his best now, so it's a fair bet he'll start in England's first game with Paraguay!

LEDLEY KING

Club: Tottenham

Position: Centre-back **Age:** 25

Debut: v Italy, 2002

King's only been in the England squad for a few years, but has proved his value with loads of top displays! Even though he's a well tough centre-back, Ledley has also played in midfield for England - and is class there too!

DAVID BECKHAM

Club: Real Madrid

Position: Midfield **Age:** 31

Debut: v Moldova, 1996

An England regular for nearly ten years, Beckham has been captain since 2000 and is closing in on 100 caps! He's played in two World Cup finals - 1998 and 2002 - and wants to lead the team to glory in 2006!

FRANK LAMPARD

Club: Chelsea

Position: Midfield **Age:** 27

Debut: v Belgium, 1999

Frank has probably been England's best player over the last two years - MATCH readers voted him Player Of The Year in 2004 and 2005! When England need to hit goals from midfield, Franky Lamps is the man!

JERMAINE JENAS

Club: Tottenham

Position: Midfield **Age:** 23

Debut: v Australia, 2003

Sven's got loads of ace players to choose from, and the midfield is the toughest area to break in to! There are tons of top-notch hopefuls waiting for a chance though, and JJ is the pick of the bunch! He's class!

STEVEN GERRARD

Club: Liverpool

Position: Midfield **Age:** 26

Debut: v Ukraine, 2000

Stevie G is a key player for England, and this is a massive tournament for him after missing the 2002 World Cup through injury. Gerrard is the ultimate midfielder - top class going forward and super tough in defence!

SHAUN WRIGHT-PHILLIPS

Club: Chelsea

Position: Winger **Age:** 24

Debut: v Ukraine, 2004

SWP didn't play as many games as he would have liked for Chelsea last season, but Sven already knows what a wicked player he is! Super quick with an explosive shot and awesome dribbling skills, Wright-Phillips rocks!

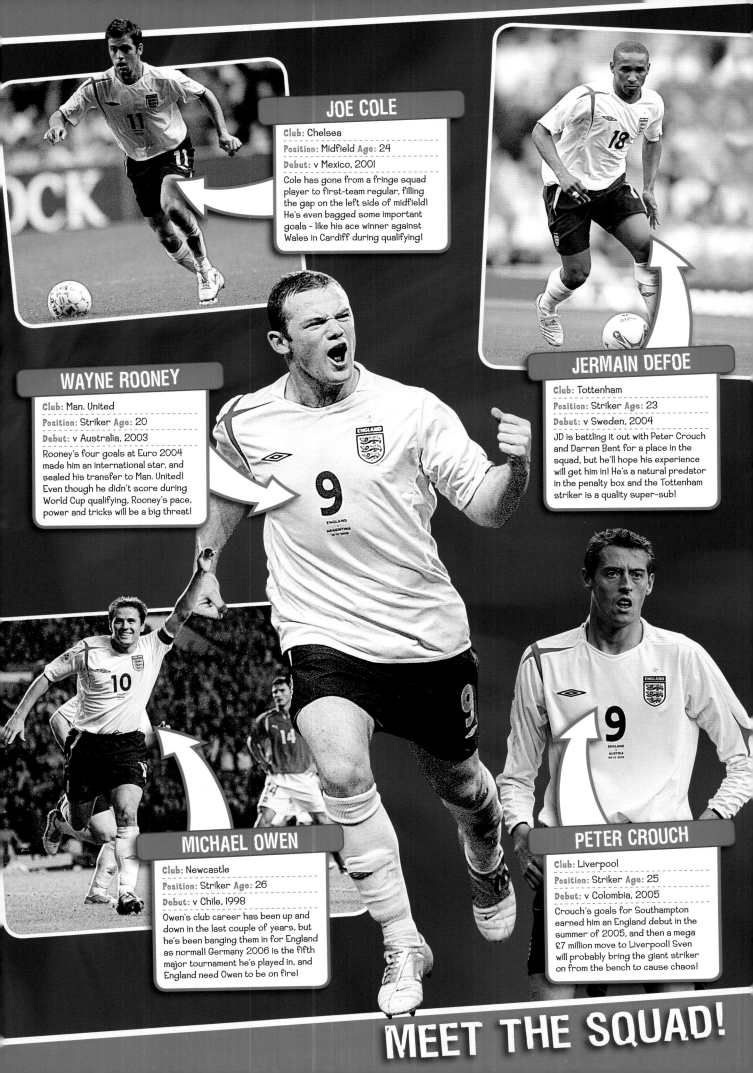

JOE COLE

Club: Chelsea

Position: Midfield **Age:** 24

Debut: v Mexico, 2001

Cole has gone from a fringe squad player to first-team regular, filling the gap on the left side of midfield! He's even bagged some important goals - like his ace winner against Wales in Cardiff during qualifying!

JERMAIN DEFOE

Club: Tottenham

Position: Striker **Age:** 23

Debut: v Sweden, 2004

JD is battling it out with Peter Crouch and Darren Bent for a place in the squad, but he'll hope his experience will get him in! He's a natural predator in the penalty box and the Tottenham striker is a quality super-sub!

WAYNE ROONEY

Club: Man. United

Position: Striker **Age:** 20

Debut: v Australia, 2003

Rooney's four goals at Euro 2004 made him an international star, and sealed his transfer to Man. United! Even though he didn't score during World Cup qualifying, Rooney's pace, power and tricks will be a big threat!

MICHAEL OWEN

Club: Newcastle

Position: Striker **Age:** 26

Debut: v Chile, 1998

Owen's club career has been up and down in the last couple of years, but he's been banging them in for England as normal! Germany 2006 is the fifth major tournament he's played in, and England need Owen to be on fire!

PETER CROUCH

Club: Liverpool

Position: Striker **Age:** 25

Debut: v Colombia, 2005

Crouch's goals for Southampton earned him an England debut in the summer of 2005, and then a mega £7 million move to Liverpool! Sven will probably bring the giant striker on from the bench to cause chaos!

MEET THE SQUAD!

RONALDO'S... WORLD CUP

RONALDO is ready to win **BRAZIL** a sixth World Cup crown and become the tournament's record goalscorer!

WHAT'S IT LIKE TO PLAY FOR A TEAM LIKE BRAZIL?

"It's the best feeling in the world! There is also a sense of great responsibility to wear the famous yellow jersey of Brazil. The pressure is huge, and the players carry that with a lot of pride and a lot of satisfaction because historically, the best players in the world played for Brazil. We are all very proud to wear the famous shirt!"

BRAZIL HAD TO QUALIFY FOR THIS WORLD CUP. WAS IT GOOD FOR THE TEAM?

"Yes, I think it actually helped us because we found a much better understanding among the players. The majority of the team play in Europe, so having qualifying games got us all together more often and kept the group united and updated with tactics."

WHO ARE THE FAVOURITES TO WIN THE WORLD CUP?

"For me, the favourites are always the traditional bigger nations. I don't really believe in surprises at the World Cup. Sometimes they happen in the group stages, but when it gets down to the knockout stages shocks don't usually happen again."

AUSTRALIA, JAPAN AND CROATIA ARE IN YOUR GROUP. WILL IT BE TOUGH?

"All three will be tough games, and I wouldn't put one ahead of another. When you get to the World Cup there are no easy games! Japan's football has really come on in recent years and they will be a strong team. Australia have a great coach in Guus Hiddink who has been at a lot of World Cups with different teams and has done great things. He got to the semi-finals the last time and he is a great manager."

WHY HAVE THE SOUTH AMERICAN TEAMS ONLY WON ONE WORLD CUP HELD IN EUROPE?

"It's been a long time without success in Europe. We were close in France '98, only for France to beat us in the final. We want to end this legend of South Americans not winning World Cups staged in Europe!"

P DREAM!

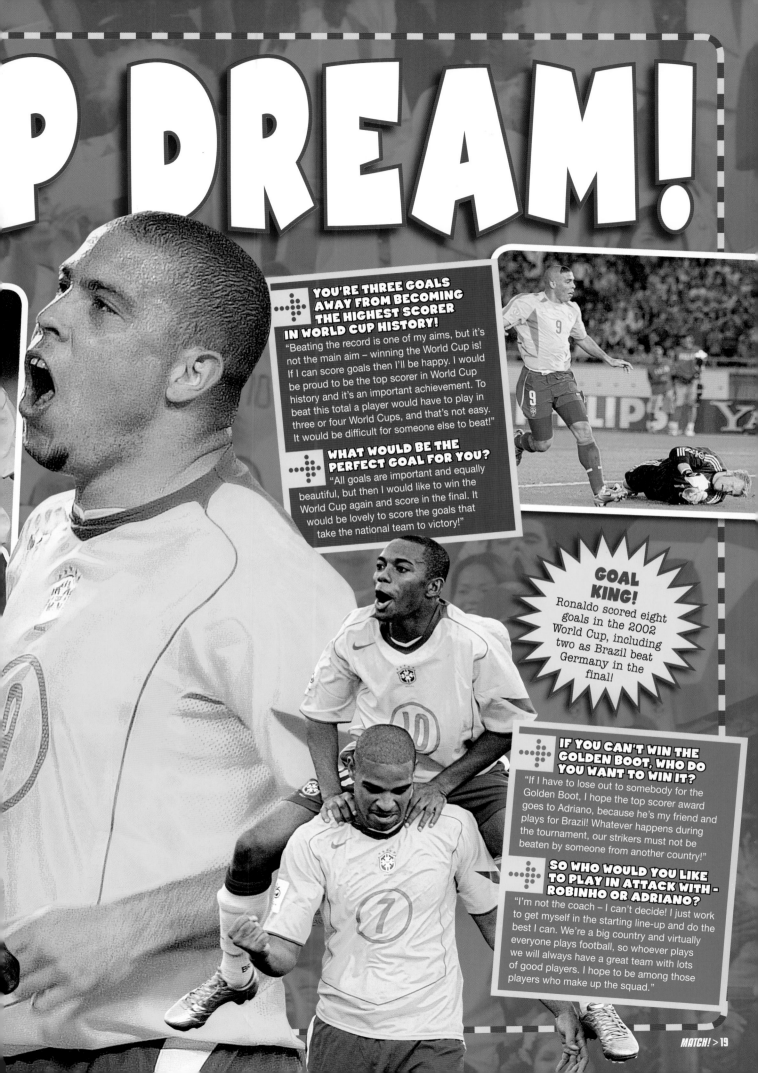

YOU'RE THREE GOALS AWAY FROM BECOMING THE HIGHEST SCORER IN WORLD CUP HISTORY!

"Beating the record is one of my aims, but it's not the main aim – winning the World Cup is! If I can score goals then I'll be happy. I would be proud to be the top scorer in World Cup history and it's an important achievement. To beat this total a player would have to play in three or four World Cups, and that's not easy. It would be difficult for someone else to beat!"

WHAT WOULD BE THE PERFECT GOAL FOR YOU?

"All goals are important and equally beautiful, but then I would like to win the World Cup again and score in the final. It would be lovely to score the goals that take the national team to victory!"

GOAL KING!
Ronaldo scored eight goals in the 2002 World Cup, including two as Brazil beat Germany in the final!

IF YOU CAN'T WIN THE GOLDEN BOOT, WHO DO YOU WANT TO WIN IT?

"If I have to lose out to somebody for the Golden Boot, I hope the top scorer award goes to Adriano, because he's my friend and plays for Brazil! Whatever happens during the tournament, our strikers must not be beaten by someone from another country!"

SO WHO WOULD YOU LIKE TO PLAY IN ATTACK WITH – ROBINHO OR ADRIANO?

"I'm not the coach – I can't decide! I just work to get myself in the starting line-up and do the best I can. We're a big country and virtually everyone plays football, so whoever plays we will always have a great team with lots of good players. I hope to be among those players who make up the squad."

GROUP B
PAGE
28

GROUP A
PAGE
22

WORLD CUP

GROUP D
PAGE
40

GROUP C
PAGE
34

2006!

Wanna know everything about the 32 teams battling for World Cup glory? Check out the ultimate **MATCH** guide to the 2006 finals!

*'ALL STATS & TEAM INFO CORRECT AS OF FEB. 22, 2006.

GERMANY!

| COACH! | JURGEN KLINSMANN | CAPTAIN! | MICHAEL BALLACK | MOST CAPS! | OLIVER KAHN 83 |

★ RECENT FORM! ★

Germany didn't have to qualify for the finals, so they've been playing friendlies for two years to prepare for the World Cup. A 1-0 home win over China, and defeats away in Turkey and Slovakia, didn't do much for their confidence. A draw against France last November was better though, and a 2-2 draw in Holland was promising.

★ STRENGTHS! ★

Germany have exciting young players desperate to make an impact! Striker Lukas Podolski has been doing the business and Bastian Schweinsteiger is a skilful midfielder. Robert Huth, Per Mertesacker, Andreas Hinkel and Thomas Hitzlsperger could become massive stars during the tournament!

★ WEAKNESSES! ★

Apart from captain Michael Ballack, Germany don't have the big-name players they need to win their fourth World Cup. Coach Jurgen Klinsmann can't just rely on his talented kids!

Miroslav Klose.

★ CAN THEY WIN? ★

Germany haven't played like potential champions for years, and there's little to say they can suddenly turn on the style. But home advantage is a huge bonus, and Germany will remember 2002 when, unfancied from the start, they went all the way to the final. It's realistic that they'll reach the quarter-finals, but it's always very dangerous to write the Germans off!

MATCHMAN'S VERDICT: "AS DA HOSTS, THERE'S PRESSURE ON GERMANY TO DO DA BIZNIZ AT HOME! ARE THEY GOOD ENOUGH TO WIN IT? NAH, I DON'T THINK SO!"

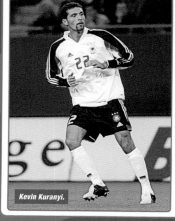

Kevin Kuranyi.

★ RESULTS AND LINE-UPS IN FRIENDLIES!

SLOVENIA	N. IRELAND	RUSSIA	HOLLAND	SLOVAKIA	SOUTH AFRICA
Won 1-0 (a)	Won 4-1 (a)	Drew 2-2 (h)	Drew 2-2 (a)	Lost 1-0 (a)	Won 4-2 (h)
Kahn	Lehmann	Kahn	Kahn	Lehmann	Lehmann
Hinkel	Owomoyela	Hinkel	Friedrich	Owomoyela	Owomoyela
Friedrich	Mertesacker	Friedrich	Mertesacker	Mertesacker	Mertesacker
Huth	Huth	Mertesacker	Worns	Worns	Sinkiewicz
Hitzlsperger	Hitzlsperger	Hitzlsperger	Schneider	Hitzlsperger	Jansen
Frings	Schneider	Schneider	Frings	Deisler	Deisler
Ballack	Ballack 2	Ballack	Hamann	Ernst	Borowski 1
Baumann	Frings	Frings	Ballack 1	Ballack	Ballack
Neuville	Ernst	Schweinsteiger 2	Ernst	Schneider	Schweinsteiger
Klose	Asamoah 1	Asamoah	Kuranyi	Klose	Klose
Podolski 1	Kuranyi	Podolski	Klose	Asamoah	Podolski 3
Substitutes:	**Substitutes:**	**Substitutes:**	**Substitutes:**	**Substitutes:**	**Substitutes:**
Schweinsteiger 59	Deisler 46	Deisler 46	Asamoah 1 46	Jansen 46	Schneider 4
Owomoyela 73	Schweinsteiger 46	Hanke 62	Deisler 46	Podolski 46	Ernst 6
Kuranyi 75	Podolski 1 63	Ernst 84	Hitzlsperger 66	Schweinsteiger 46	Kuranyi 7
Borowski 84	Borowski 73	Kuranyi 84	Huth 66	Sinkiewicz 46	Asamoah 7
			Borowski 74	Hinkel 74	
			Hinkel 74	Kuranyi 82	

MOST GOALS!	MICHAEL BALLACK 29	WORLD RANKING!	17TH	WORLD CUP ODDS!	13/2	WORLD CUP BEST!	WINNERS 1954, 1974, 1990

PLAYER TO WATCH!

Sebastian Deisler

Deisler has bounced back well from a serious knee injury and illness to recapture his form. He's Germany's David Beckham – playing on the right wing, Deisler's a brilliant crosser and free-kick taker!

STRONGEST STARTING LINE-UP! 4-4-2

KAHN

FRIEDRICH — MERTESACKER — WORNS — JANSEN

DEISLER — BALLACK — FRINGS — SCHWEINSTEIGER

PODOLSKI — KURANYI

THE PLAYERS!

GOALKEEPERS
Timo Hildebrand	Stuttgart
Oliver Kahn	Bayern Munich
Jens Lehmann	Arsenal

DEFENDERS
Arne Friedrich	Hertha Berlin
Andreas Hinkel	Stuttgart
Thomas Hitzlsperger	Aston Villa
Robert Huth	Chelsea
Marcell Jansen	Borussia M'gladbach
Phillip Lahm	Bayern Munich
Per Mertesacker	Hanover
Christoph Metzelder	Borussia Dortmund
Patrick Owomoyela	Werder Bremen
Lukas Sinkiewicz	Cologne
Christian Worns	Borussia Dortmund

MIDFIELDERS
Michael Ballack	Bayern Munich
Tim Borowski	Werder Bremen
Sebastian Deisler	Bayern Munich
Fabian Ernst	Schalke
Torsten Frings	Werder Bremen
Dietmar Hamann	Liverpool
Sebastian Kehl	Borussia Dortmund
Bernd Schneider	Bayer Leverkusen
Bastian Schweinsteiger	Bayern Munich

STRIKERS
Gerald Asamoah	Schalke
Mike Hanke	Wolfsburg
Kevin Kuranyi	Schalke
Miroslav Klose	Werder Bremen
Oliver Neuville	Borussia M'gladbach
Lukas Podolski	Cologne

Oliver Kahn.

PLAYER TO WATCH!

Bastian Schweinsteiger

A gifted midfielder who caught the eye for Germany at Euro 2004, Schweinsteiger combines hard work with neat passing. The 21-year-old chips in with important goals too – he's a rising star of German footy!

TURKEY	CHINA	FRANCE
Lost 2-1 (a)	Won 1-0 (h)	Drew 0-0 (a)
n	Kahn	Lehmann
omoyela	Friedrich	Friedrich
rtesacker	Mertesacker	Mertesacker
kiewicz	Metzelder	Huth
nsen	Deisler	Jansen
hneider	Schneider	Deisler
ngs	Frings 1	Frings
rowski	Borowski	Ballack
hweinsteiger	Schweinsteiger	Schneider
dolski	Neuville	Klose
ranyi	Podolski	Podolski

Substitutes:		Substitutes:		Substitutes:	
ngs	46	Huth	46	Schweinsteiger	46
uville 1	46	Kuranyi	52	Borowski	76
nke	73	Hitzlsperger	89	Kuranyi	83
tzlsperger	82	Owomoyela	90		

Michael Ballack.

POLAND!

COACH!	PAWEL JANAS	WORLD RANKING!	23RD	WORLD CUP ODDS!	100/1	WORLD CUP BEST!	THIRD 1974, 1982

Tomasz Frankowski.

Jacek Krzynowek.

THE PLAYERS!

GOALKEEPERS

Artur Boruc	Celtic
Jerzy Dudek	Liverpool
Wojciech Kowalewski	Spartak Moscow

DEFENDERS

Jacek Bak	Al Rayan
Marcin Baszczynski	Wisla Krakow
Dariusz Dudka	Wisla Krakow
Arkadius Glowacki	Wisla Krakow
Mariusz Jop	FC Moscow
Tomasz Klos	Wisla Krakow
Tomasz Rzasa	Den Haag
Michael Zewlakow	Anderlecht
Marcin Wasilewski	Amica Wronki

MIDFIELDERS

Marcin Kaczmarek	Kolporter Korona Kielce
Kamil Kosowski	Southampton
Jacek Krzynowek	Bayer Leverkusen
Mariusz Lewandowski	Shakhtar Donetsk
Sebastian Mila	Austria Vienna
Arkadiusz Radomski	Austria Vienna
Euzebiusz Smolarek	Borussia Dortmund
Radoslav Sobolewski	Wisla Krakow
Miroslav Szymkowiak	Trabzonspor

STRIKERS

Pawel Brozek	Wisla Krakow
Tomasz Frankowski	Elche
Andrzej Niedzielan	NEC Nijmegen
Gregorz Rasiak	Tottenham
Maciej Zurawski	Celtic

STRONGEST STARTING LINE-UP! 4-4-2

BORUC

KLOS — BASZCZYNSKI — BAK — ZEWLAKOW

SMOLAREK — SZYMKOWIAK — KOSOWSKI — KRZYNOWEK

ZURAWSKI — FRANKOWSKI

TEAMTALK!

Poland qualified as one of the two best second-placed teams in Europe, but their record was impressive and they only just missed out on topping their group ahead of England. With eight wins from ten games, the Poles were beaten twice – both 2-1 defeats to England – but scored ten more goals than The Three Lions. Coach Pawel Janas loves to attack, and his team will always score goals. Maciej Zurawski, Tomasz Frankowski, Jacek Kryznowek and Gregorz Rasiak are the danger guys in the box!

MATCHMAN'S VERDICT: "AFTER PUSHING ENGLAND HARD IN DA QUALIFIERS, POLAND WANNA KICK ON AND REACH DA KNOCKOUT STAGES!"

PLAYER TO WATCH!

Maciej Zurawski

Poland scored loads in qualifying, and Zurawski bagged seven in a deadly partnership with Tomasz Frankowski. The Celtic striker notched against England, and his penalty at home to Wales sealed Poland's World Cup spot!

Kami Kosowski.

WORLD CUP FINALS 2006 — GROUP A

COSTA RICA!

| COACH! | ALEXANDRE GUIMARAES | WORLD RANKING! | 21ST | WORLD CUP ODDS! | 500/1 | WORLD CUP BEST! | SECOND ROUND 1990 |

STRONGEST STARTING LINE-UP! 4-4-2

PORRAS

DRUMMOND · MARTINEZ · UMANA · MARIN

SABORIO · CENTENO · M SOLIS · HERNANDEZ

WANCHOPE · GOMEZ

TEAMTALK!

Costa Rica looked like they would never qualify for the World Cup until a change of coach resulted in a change of luck! When Alexandre Guimaraes became the new boss, 'Los Ticos' then beat Guatemala and Panama before two victories over Trinidad & Tobago and the USA booked their place at Germany 2006. This will be Costa Rica's third World Cup tournament and, led by former Man. City striker Paulo Wanchope, don't be shocked if they go on to land a place in the second round!

MATCHMAN'S VERDICT: "COSTA RICA ARE WELL UP FOR THE WORLD CUP AND WANNA UPSET GERMANY IN THE FIRST GAME!"

PLAYER TO WATCH!

Gilberto Martinez
Martinez holds Costa Rica's defence together, and he's one of the nation's best-ever players after spending many seasons in Italy with Brescia. He can play anywhere across the back four, but is at his best at centre-back.

ROAD TO THE FINALS!

Stage 2 Group 2	P	W	D	L	F	A	Pts
Costa Rica	6	3	1	2	2	8	0
Guatemala	6	3	1	2	7	9	10
Honduras	6	1	4	1	9	7	7
Canada	6	1	2	3	4	8	5

Stage 3	P	W	D	L	F	A	Pts
USA	10	7	1	2	6	2	—
Mexico	10	7	1	2	22	22	—
Costa Rica	10	5	1	4	15	14	16
Trinidad & Tobago	10	4	1	5	10	15	13
Guatemala	10	3	2	5	16	18	11
Panama	10	0	2	8	4	21	2

RESULT	SCORE	OPPOSITION	H/A
Drew	2-2	Cuba	A
Drew	1-1	Cuba	H
Lost	5-2	Honduras	H
Lost	2-1	Guatemala	H
Won	1-0	Canada	H
Won	5-0	Guatemala	H
Won	3-1	Canada	A
Drew	0-0	Honduras	A
Lost	2-1	Mexico	H
Won	2-1	Panama	H
Drew	0-0	Trinidad & Tobago	A
Lost	3-0	USA	A
Won	3-2	Guatemala	H
Lost	2-0	Mexico	A
Won	3-1	Panama	A
Won	2-0	Trinidad & Tobago	H
Won	3-0	USA	H
Lost	3-1	Guatemala	A

TOP SCORERS	
Paulo Wanchope	8
Carlos Hernandez	5

ECUADOR!

| COACH! | LUIS HERNANDO SUAREZ | WORLD RANKING! | 38TH | WORLD CUP ODDS! | 300/1 | WORLD CUP BEST! | FIRST ROUND 2002 |

STRONGEST STARTING LINE-UP! 4-4-2

VILLAFUERTE

DE LA CRUZ · HURTADO · ESPINOSA · AMBROSSI

VALENCIA · LARA · TENDORIO · MENDEZ

DELGADO · KAVIEDES

TEAMTALK!

With qualifying wins over Brazil and Argentina, Ecuador's confidence is sky-high! The team has plenty of international experience – captain Ivan Hurtado has over 100 caps while Ulises de la Cruz, Edwin Tenorio, Marlon Ayovi, Edison Mendez and Agustin Delgado are established at this level. But the team does lack experience against European sides – a friendly in Poland last year was only their third ever full international in Europe! If Ecuador settle quickly, they'll give their rivals a fright.

MATCHMAN'S VERDICT: "ECUADOR BEAT BRAZIL AN' ARGENTINA IN QUALIFYING, BUT PLAYIN' IN EUROPE WILL BE TOUGH FOR 'EM!"

PLAYER TO WATCH!

Edison Mendez
Edison Mendez could be Ecuador's key man! He's an exciting midfielder with an eye for goal – he scored a brilliant winner against Brazil in the qualifying stages – and can play on either wing or in a central role behind the strikers.

ROAD TO THE FINALS!

South America	P	W	D	L	F	A	Pts
Brazil	18	9	7	2	35	17	34
Argentina	18	10	4	4	29	17	34
Ecuador	18	8	4	6	23	19	28
Paraguay	18	8	4	6	23	23	28
Uruguay	18	6	7	5	23	28	25
Colombia	18	6	6	6	24	16	24
Chile	18	5	7	6	18	22	22
Venezuela	18	5	3	10	20	28	18
Peru	18	4	6	8	20	28	18
Bolivia	18	4	2	12	20	37	14

RESULT	SCORE	OPPOSITION	H/A
Won	2-0	Venezuela	H
Lost	1-0	Brazil	A
Lost	2-1	Paraguay	A
Drew	0-0	Peru	H
Lost	1-0	Argentina	A
Won	2-1	Colombia	H
Won	3-2	Bolivia	H
Lost	1-0	Uruguay	A
Won	2-0	Chile	H
Lost	3-1	Venezuela	A
Won	1-0	Brazil	H
Won	5-2	Paraguay	H
Drew	2-2	Peru	A
Won	2-0	Argentina	H
Lost	3-0	Colombia	A
Won	2-1	Bolivia	A
Drew	0-0	Uruguay	H
Drew	0-0	Chile	A

TOP SCORERS	
Agustin Delgado	5
Edison Mendez	5

EXTREME SHOTS!

Argentina defender Martin Demichelis must have used a trampoline to hit this shot!

GOOD EFFORT, LAD!

GERMANY'S...
SUPER STADIUMS!

The action in Germany takes place in these awesome arenas! Check out our mega stats on all 12 World Cup stadiums!

GELSENKIRCHEN
STADIUM: AUFSCHALKE ARENA

Capacity: 52,000 fans

First game: Poland v Ecuador, June 9

STADIUM MEGA FACT: There's a three-mile long pipeline that will supply thirsty fans with drinks!

Capacity: 67,000 fans

First game: Trinidad & Tobago v Sweden, June 10

STADIUM MEGA FACT: An old bomb was found under the pitch! Crazy!

DORTMUND
STADIUM: SIGNAL IDUNA PARK

Capacity: 51,000 fans

First game: Angola v Portugal, June 11

STADIUM MEGA FACT: It's been demolished and rebuilt ready for the WC, which cost £75 million!

COLOGNE
STADIUM: RHEIN ENERGIE STADION

FRANKFURT
STADIUM: COMMERZBANK ARENA

Capacity: 48,000 fans

First game: England v Paraguay, June 10

STADIUM MEGA FACT: As well as proper footy, American football games were played here too!

KAISERSLAUTERN
STADIUM: FRITZ WALTER STADION

Capacity: 48,500 fans

First game: Australia v Japan, June 12

STADIUM MEGA FACT: It's named after striker Fritz Walter, who used to play for Kaiserslautern!

MILES BETTER!

Check out how far these countries have to fly to get to Germany!

AUSTRALIA
10,198 miles

ARGENTINA
7,133 miles

JAPAN
5,838 miles

SOUTH KOREA
5,372 miles

TRINIDAD & TOBAGO
4,892 miles

HANNOVER
STADIUM: AWD ARENA

Capacity: 50,000 fans

First game: Argentina v Ivory Coast, June 10

STADIUM MEGA FACT: The ground can hold 55,000, but it's reduced for internationals!

Capacity: 49,000 fans

First game: Italy v Ghana, June 12

STADIUM MEGA FACT: The local people used to call the old floodlights 'toothbrushes'! Ha, ha!

HAMBURG
STADIUM: AOL ARENA

BERLIN
STADIUM: OLYMPIA STADION

Capacity: 76,000 fans

First game: Brazil v Croatia, June 13

STADIUM MEGA FACT: This was first used in the 1936 Olympics! That was absolutely yonks ago!

Capacity: 44,500 fans

First game: Serbia-Montenegro v Holland, June 11

STADIUM MEGA FACT: This cool ground used to hold 100,000 supporters!

Capacity: 44,000 fans

First game: Mexico v Iran, June 11

STADIUM MEGA FACT: It's been improved, but this is still the World Cup's smallest venue!

LEIPZIG
STADIUM: ZENTRAL STADION

NUREMBURG
STADIUM: FRANKEN STADION

MUNICH
STADIUM: ALLIANZ ARENA

Capacity: 51,000 fans

First game: France v Switzerland, June 13

STADIUM MEGA FACT: This cool stadium also has the two biggest TV screens in Europe!

Capacity: 66,000 fans

First game: Germany v Costa Rica, June 9

STADIUM MEGA FACT: The Allianz Arena cost a whopping £190 million to build! Woah!

STUTTGART
STADIUM: GOTTLIEB-DAIMLER STADION

ENGLAND!

COACH!	SVEN GORAN ERIKSSON
CAPTAIN!	DAVID BECKHAM
MOST CAPS!	DAVID BECKHAM 86

⭐ QUALIFYING FORM! ⭐

England's fans aren't easy to please, and one or two results worried them! Chucking away a 2-0 lead in Austria was a bad way to start the campaign, and a 1-0 defeat in Northern Ireland was poor. But England still topped their group and a 3-2 friendly win over Argentina was a big boost!

⭐ STRENGTHS! ⭐

In Wayne Rooney and Michael Owen, England have two world-class strikers. Li'l MO's scored in every tournament he's played in and Rooney can magic a goal out of nothing! England also have options in central defence, with Ferdinand, Terry, Campbell, King, Carragher and Woodgate all top class.

⭐ WEAKNESSES! ⭐

Sven has yet to find the best mix of players in midfield. Can Gerrard and Lampard both play together? Should a more defensive, holding player be used? Is Beckham best wide right, or in the middle? It's tough to decide!

Ashley Cole.

⭐ CAN THEY WIN? ⭐

This is England's best chance of World Cup glory for years! The starting X1 is strong with stars like John Terry, David Beckham and Wayne Rooney enjoying fine seasons for their clubs. There are good players lining up in reserve, too. The draw has been kind and England will want to win Group B and avoid Germany in the second round. After that, anything's possible!

MATCHMAN'S VERDICT:
"ENGLAND FANS 'AVE BEEN SAYING FOR YEARS DAT DEY SHOULD WIN THE WORLD CUP AGAIN! LET'S DO IT, BOYS!"

Rio Ferdinand.

⭐ RESULTS AND LINE-UPS IN QUALIFYING!

AUSTRIA	POLAND	WALES	AZERBAIJAN	N IRELAND	AZERBAIJAN
Drew 2-2 (a)	Won 2-1* (a)	Won 2-0 (h)	Won 1-0 (a)	Won 4-0 (h)	Won 2-0 (h)
James	Robinson	Robinson	Robinson	Robinson	Robinson
G Neville	G Neville	G Neville	G Neville	G Neville	G Neville
A Cole	A Cole	A Cole	A Cole	A Cole	A Cole
Terry	Terry	Ferdinand	Ferdinand	Ferdinand	Ferdinand
King	King	Campbell	Campbell	Terry	Terry
Beckham	Beckham	Beckham 1	Jenas	Beckham	Beckham 1
Lampard 1	Lampard	Lampard 1	Lampard	Lampard 1	Lampard
Gerrard 1	Gerrard	Butt	Butt	Gerrard	Gerrard 1
Bridge	Bridge	Rooney	Rooney	J Cole 1	J Cole
Smith	Defoe 1	Defoe	Defoe	Rooney	Rooney
Owen	Owen	Owen	Owen 1	Owen 2	Owen
Substitutes:	**Substitutes:**	**Substitutes:**	**Substitutes:**	**Substitutes:**	**Substitutes:**
Defoe 76	Carragher 30	Smith 70	Smith 55	Dyer 72	King
Carragher 82	Dyer 87	Hargreaves 85	Wright-Phillip 72	Hargreaves 72	Dyer
J Cole 84	Hargreaves 89	King 87	J Cole 85	Defoe 81	Defoe

WORLD CUP FINALS 2006 GROUP B

MOST GOALS!	MICHAEL OWEN 35	WORLD RANKING!	9TH	WORLD CUP ODDS!	7/1	WORLD CUP BEST!	WINNERS 1966

⭐ PLAYER TO WATCH! ⭐

Frank Lampard

Lampard wasn't in England's squad for the 2002 World Cup, but in the last few seasons the Chelsea star has become priceless for club and country! A complete midfielder, Lamps scores plenty of goals too!

⭐ PLAYER TO WATCH! ⭐

Michael Owen

Owen should be fully fit and raring to go after suffering a broken foot playing for Newcastle. He proved what a danger he is in the box with two late goals in the 3-2 friendly victory over Argentina last year!

⭐ STRONGEST STARTING LINE-UP! 4-4-2

ROBINSON

G NEVILLE — FERDINAND — TERRY — A COLE

BECKHAM — GERRARD — LAMPARD — J COLE

OWEN — ROONEY

⭐ ROAD TO THE FINALS! ⭐

Group 6 Europe	P	W	D	L	F	A	Pts
England	10	8	1	1	17	5	25
Poland	10	8	0	2	27	9	24
Austria	10	4	3	3	15	12	15
N. Ireland	10	2	3	5	10	18	9
Wales	10	2	2	6	10	15	8
Azerbaijan	10	0	3	7	1	21	3

TOP SCORERS	
Frank Lampard	5
Michael Owen	4
Beckham, Joe Cole, Gerrard	2

David Beckham.

⭐ THE PLAYERS! ⭐

GOALKEEPERS	
Robert Green	Norwich
David James	Man. City
Paul Robinson	Tottenham

DEFENDERS	
Wayne Bridge	Chelsea
Sol Campbell	Arsenal
Jamie Carragher	Liverpool
Ashley Cole	Arsenal
Rio Ferdinand	Man. United
Ledley King	Tottenham
Gary Neville	Man. United
John Terry	Chelsea
Jonathan Woodgate	Real Madrid
Luke Young	Charlton

MIDFIELDERS	
David Beckham	Real Madrid
Michael Carrick	Tottenham
Joe Cole	Chelsea
Steven Gerrard	Liverpool
Owen Hargreaves	Bayern Munich
Jermaine Jenas	Tottenham
Frank Lampard	Chelsea
Kieran Richardson	Man. United
Shaun Wright-Phillips	Chelsea

STRIKERS	
Peter Crouch	Liverpool
Jermain Defoe	Tottenham
Michael Owen	Newcastle
Wayne Rooney	Man. United

Rooney & Owen.

Steven Gerrard.

	WALES	N. IRELAND	AUSTRIA	POLAND
	Won 1-0 (a)	Lost 1-0 (a)	Won 1-0 (h)	Won 2-1 (h)
...binson	Robinson	Robinson	Robinson	Robinson
...ng	Young	Young	Young	Young
...ole	A Cole	Ferdinand	Carragher	Carragher
...dinand	Ferdinand	Terry	Terry	Ferdinand
...ragher	Carragher	Campbell	Campbell	Terry
...ght-Phillips	Wright-Phillips	Wright-Phillips	Beckham	Wright-Phillips
...ckham	Beckham	Beckham	Lampard 1	Lampard 1
...pard	Lampard	Lampard	Gerrard	King
...rrard	Gerrard	Gerrard	J Cole	J Cole
...le 1	Rooney	J Cole	Crouch	Rooney
...oney	Owen	Rooney	Owen	Owen 1
Substitutes:	**Substitutes:**	**SUBSTITUTES:**	**SUBSTITUTES:**	**Substitutes:**
...oe 68	J Cole 53	King 62	Crouch 67	
...greaves 77	Defoe 75	Ferdinand 65	Jenas 84	
...hardson 84	Hargreaves 80	Richardson 80	Smith 87	

SWEDEN!

COACH!	LARS LAGERBACK	WORLD RANKING!	14TH	WORLD CUP ODDS!	33/1	WORLD CUP BEST!	RUNNERS-UP 1958

Freddie Ljungberg.

ROAD TO THE FINALS!

Group 8 Europe	P	W	D	L	F	A	Pts
Croatia	10	7	3	0	21	5	24
Sweden	10	8	0	2	30	4	24
Bulgaria	10	4	3	3	17	17	15
Hungary	10	4	2	4	13	14	14
Iceland	10	1	1	8	14	27	4
Malta	10	3	0	7	4	32	3

RESULT	SCORE	OPPOSITION	H/A
Won	7-0	Malta	A
Lost	1-0	Croatia	H
Won	3-0	Hungary	H
Won	4-1	Iceland	A
Won	3-0	Bulgaria	A
Won	6-0	Malta	H
Won	3-0	Bulgaria	H
Won	1-0	Hungary	A
Lost	1-0	Croatia	A
Won	3-1	Iceland	H

TOP SCORERS

Zlatan Ibrahimovic	8
Freddie Ljungberg	7
Henrik Larsson	5

Ibrahimovic & Larsson.

STRONGEST STARTING LINE-UP! 4-4-2

ISAKSSON

OSTLUND — MELLBERG — LUCIC — EDMAN

WILHELMSSON — LINDEROTH — KALLSTROM — LJUNGBERG

IBRAHIMOVIC — LARSSON

THE PLAYERS!

GOALKEEPERS	
John Alvbage	Viborg
Eddie Gustafsson	Ham-Kam
Andreas Isaksson	Rennes

DEFENDERS	
Christopher Andersson	Lillestrom
Matias Concha	Djurgarden
Eric Edman	Rennes
Michael Dorsin	Rosenborg
Andreas Granqvist	Helsingborg
Teddy Lucic	BK Haecken
Olof Mellberg	Aston Villa
Mikael Nilsson	Panathinaikos
Olof Persson	Malmo

MIDFIELDERS	
Niclas Alexandersson	IFK Gothenburg
Johan Arneng	Djurgarden
Dusan Djuric	Halmstad
Martin Ericsson	Aalborg
Kim Kallstrom	Rennes
Tobias Linderoth	Copenhagen
Freddie Ljungberg	Arsenal
Anders Svensson	Elfsborg
Karl Svensson	IFK Gothenburg
Christian Wilhelmsson	Anderlecht

STRIKERS	
Marcus Allback	Copenhagen
Johan Elmander	Brondby
Zlatan Ibrahimovic	Juventus
Mattias Jonson	Djurgarden
Henrik Larsson	Barcelona
Yksel Osmanovski	Malmo
Markus Rosenberg	Ajax
Stefan Selakovic	IFK Gothenburg

TEAMTALK!

Sweden were pretty solid through the qualifying campaign, and although they were beaten twice – both times 1-0 by group winners Croatia – their overall record saw them through as one of Europe's best runners-up.
It would still be a massive surprise if Sweden won the World Cup, but with class attacking players like Zlatan Ibrahimovic, Freddie Ljungberg and Henrik Larsson they will be dark horses and should make the second round. If all goes to plan, they will play Germany after the group stage!

PLAYER TO WATCH!

Christian Wilhelmsson
Wicked winger Wilhemsson was one of Sweden's biggest stars at Euro 2004! The 26-year-old has kept his place in the national squad ever since and his silky skills have seen him linked with a big move to the Premiership!

MATCHMAN'S VERDICT:
"A STRONG TEAM SPIRIT AND A DEADLY STRIKEFORCE MAKES SUPER SWEDEN A MATCH FOR ANYONE DIS SUMMER!"

PARAGUAY!

COACH!	ANIBAL RUIZ	WORLD RANKING!	30TH	WORLD CUP ODDS!	250/1	WORLD CUP BEST!	SECOND ROUND 1986, 1998, 2002

★ STRONGEST STARTING LINE-UP! 4-4-2

GOMEZ

NUNEZ — GAMARRA — CACERES — FATECHA

ACUNA — MONTIEL — DA SILVA — CANIZA

HAEDO VALDEZ — SANTA CRUZ

★ TEAMTALK!

Drawn in the same group as England and Sweden, Paraguay coach Anibal Ruiz is still confident of success. In qualifying they beat Argentina, held Brazil at home and gave Uruguay a 4-1 thrashing, so they're dangerous opponents for the Europeans. With strikers Haedo Valdez, Jose Cardozo and Roque Santa Cruz – who is hoping to fit after a knee injury – there is plenty of attacking quality to choose from and the defence is marshalled by the superb Carlos Gamarra. They're a decent team!

MATCHMAN'S VERDICT: "DON'T WRITE OFF PARAGUAY – THE SOUTH AMERICANS HAVE SOME DANGEROUS DUDES WHO COULD MAKE A REAL IMPACT!"

★ PLAYER TO WATCH!

Nelson Haedo Valdez
Valdez knows his way around Germany – he plays for Werder Bremen in the Bundesliga – and the striker did his bit to get Paraguay to the finals. He helped his team beat Argentina and scored the vital winner against Venezuela!

★ ROAD TO THE FINALS!

South America	P	W	D	L	F	A	Pts
Brazil	18	9	7	2	35	17	34
Argentina	18	10	4	4	29	17	34
Eduador	18	8	4	6	23	19	28
Paraguay	18	8	4	6	23	23	28
Uruguay	18	6	7	5	23	28	25
Colombia	18	6	6	6	24	16	24
Chile	18	5	7	6	18	22	22
Venezuela	18	5	3	10	20	28	18
Peru	18	4	6	8	20	28	18
Bolivia	18	4	2	12	20	37	14

RESULT	SCORE	OPPOSITION	H/A
Lost	4-1	Peru	A
Won	4-1	Uruguay	H
Won	2-1	Ecuador	H
Won	1-0	Chile	A
Drew	0-0	Brazil	H
Lost	2-1	Bolivia	A
Drew	0-0	Argentina	A
Won	1-0	Venezuela	H
Drew	1-1	Colombia	A
Drew	1-1	Peru	H
Lost	1-0	Uruguay	A
Lost	5-2	Ecuador	A
Won	2-1	Chile	H
Lost	4-1	Brazil	A
Won	4-1	Bolivia	H
Won	1-0	Argentina	H
Won	1-0	Venezuela	A
Lost	1-0	Colombia	H

TOP SCORERS	
Jose Cardozo	7
Roque Santa Cruz	4

TRINIDAD & TOBAGO!

COACH!	LEO BEENHAKKER	WORLD RANKING!	50TH	WORLD CUP ODDS!	1000/1	WORLD CUP BEST!	DEBUT IN FINALS

★ STRONGEST STARTING LINE-UP! 4-4-2

WARNER

A. JOHN — ANDREWS — LAWRENCE — WHITLEY

EDWARDS — BIRCHALL — LATAPY — GRAY

JOHN — YORKE

★ TEAMTALK!

Trinidad & Tobago created history to grab a place in the World Cup finals for the first time! The little Caribbean nation struggled to qualify at first, but when coach Leo Beenhakker took charge, the team hit top form. Many of their players are familiar to UK fans – captain Dwight Yorke, Stern John, Shaka Hislop and Tony Warner have Premiership experience, while Marvin Andrews and Russell Latapy have been big hits in Scottish football. It will be tough in Germany, but you can bet Trinidad & Tobago will love it!

MATCHMAN'S VERDICT: "TRINIDAD & TOBAGO PULLED OFF A MEGA MIRACLE TO QUALIFY FOR THE WORLD CUP, AND ARE OUT TO SPRING A SURPRISE OR TWO!"

★ PLAYER TO WATCH!

Dwight Yorke
Former Man. United hitman Yorke is T&T's best player ever, and playing in his first World Cup finals is a great way to finish off his glittering career. The captain links up very well with Coventry City striker Stern John.

★ ROAD TO THE FINALS!

Stage 2 Group 3	P	W	D	L	F	A	Pts
Mexico	6	6	0	0	27	1	18
Trinidad & Tobago	6	4	0	2	12	9	12
St. Vincent/Gren.	6	2	0	4	5	12	6
St Kitts & Nevis	6	0	0	6	2	24	0

Stage 3	P	W	D	L	F	A	Pts
USA	10	7	1	2	16	6	22
Mexico	10	7	1	2	22	9	22
Costa Rica	10	5	1	4	15	14	16
Trinidad & Tobago	10	4	1	5	10	15	13
Guatemala	10	3	2	5	16	18	11
Panama	10	0	2	8	4	21	2

RESULT	SCORE	OPPOSITION	H/A
Won	2-0	Dominican Republic	A
Won	4-0	Dominican Republic	H
Won	2-0	St Vincent/Grenadines	A
Won	2-1	St Kitts & Nevis	A
Lost	3-1	Mexico	H
Won	5-1	St Kitts & Nevis	H
Lost	3-0	Mexico	A
Won	2-1	St Vincent/Grenadines	H
Lost	2-1	USA	H
Lost	5-1	Guatemala	A
Drew	0-0	Costa Rica	H
Won	2-0	Panama	A
Lost	2-0	Mexico	H
Lost	1-0	USA	A
Won	3-2	Guatemala	H
Lost	1-0	Costa Rica	A
Won	1-0	Panama	H
Won	2-1	Mexico	H
Drew	1-1	Bahrain (play-off)	H
Won	1-0	Bahrain (play-off)	A

TOP SCORER	
Stern John	12

MATCHY'S FOOTY FITTIES!

HI MATCHY, DO YA WANNA HUG?

TWO WORLD CUPS!

The World Cup winners will lift only the second trophy in the tournament's history! The first, called the Jules Rimet, was given to Brazil in 1970 after they won their third World Cup final!

THE OLD JULES RIMET CUP!

THE CURRENT WORLD CUP!

Yep, I'm only a baby MATCH!

YOUNGEST-EVER PLAYER!

Norman Whiteside became the youngest player in World Cup history when he made his debut for Northern Ireland at the 1982 finals, aged 17 years and 42 days!

MOST WINNERS' MEDALS!

Brazil megastar Pele is the World Cup's most successful player ever – lifting the trophy three times! But Cafu will be level with him if Brazil are winners this summer!

And I only wore one boot, look!

RECORD BREAK

Over the years, all sorts of amazing footy records have made the World Cup history books! Take a look at the best of the footy stats!

Blink and you'll miss it!

FASTEST GOAL!

Hakan Sukur scored for Turkey against South Korea after only 11 seconds in their 2002 play-off game. That's fast!

MOST WORLD CUP APPEARANCES!

Antonio Carbajal is the only star to have played in five World Cups! He was Mexico's goalkeeper in the 1950, '54, '58, '62 and '66 finals! Wicked, eh?

NICE HAIR, GERD!

MOST CAREER WORLD CUP GOALS!

West Germany's Gerd Muller hit 14 goals at the 1970 and '74 finals, making him the highest scorer so far! Brazil's Ronaldo needs just three goals to beat that!

IVORY COAST THE ELEPHANTS!

MOOOO!

NO KOLO, WE'RE ELEPHANTS!

BAAAAH!

Er, where is everyone?

THE WRONG SEAT!

This France fan is a bit confused!

HIGHEST-SCORING MATCH!

There were 12 mega goals when Austria played Switzerland in the 1954 finals! The final score was 7-5 to Austria! Mad!

AUSTRIA........7
SWITZERLAND...5

MOST GOALS IN ONE TOURNAMENT!

France striker Just Fontaine was a right score-o-saurus! He bagged a whopping 12 goals during the 1958 finals!

BIGGEST CROWD!

Check this – 199,854 fans packed into Rio de Janeiro's Maracana Stadium to watch the 1950 World Cup final between Brazil and Uruguay!

...ERS!

OLDEST WORLD CUP WINNER!

Legendary Italy 'keeper Dino Zoff was an ancient 41 years old when he led Italy to World Cup glory in 1982!

Woah, I'm shattered!

penalty kings...

Every team practises pens, but some are good from the spot, and some ain't! See who rocks and who sucks in shoot-outs!

...and CLOWNS!

penalty kings!

1. germany - 3 wins!
2. argentina - 3 wins!
3. france - 2 wins!

penalty clowns!

1. italy - 3 defeats!
2. mexico - 2 defeats!
3. england - 2 defeats!

HANGIN' WITH THE REFS!

These guys really know how to have a good time! Take a look at what the World Cup's top referees get up to when they're not messing up the footy!

Right, I'm off to clean my car!

Votching zis brick wall ist vunderbar!

Graham Poll England

Splendid. I will now arrange my socks!

Markus Merk Germany

Valentin Ivanov Russia

ARGENTINA!

| COACH! | JOSE PEKERMAN | CAPTAIN! | JUAN PABLO SORIN | MOST CAPS! | JAVIER ZANETTI 105 |

★ QUALIFYING FORM! ★

Argentina's early qualifying form was patchy, but the team recovered from a change of coach – Jose Pekerman stepped in after Marcelo Bielsa quit – to secure a place in the finals. With ten wins in their 18 games, Argentina booked a spot with an impressive 3-1 win against deadly rivals Brazil!

★ STRENGTHS! ★

Coach Pekerman has so many exciting attacking players to choose from, he's spoilt for choice! Lionel Messi, Juan Riquelme, Carlos Tevez, Pablo Aimar and Javier Saviola will all fight it out to supply star striker Hernan Crespo. How do you fit them all in one team?

★ WEAKNESSES! ★

Argentina's biggest problem could be nothing to do with players or tactics – but that the tournament is being held in Europe! The South American teams have struggled in Europe – only Brazil have won it here, back in 1958 – so they'll have to create history in 2006!

Javier Saviola.

★ CAN THEY WIN? ★

Yes! With the quality of players and their skills on the pitch, Argentina are probably only second to Brazil. But having star names means little in World Cup footy, and Argentina won't forget what happened in 2002, when the team was knocked out in the group stages. Argentina need to be on top form just to get out of this group ahead of Holland.

MATCHMAN'S VERDICT: "WOW! CHECK SOME OF DA NAMES ON DA ARGIE TEAMSHEET! I RECKON THEY'RE RIGHT UP THERE WITH BRAZIL AND ENGLAND!"

★ RESULTS AND LINE-UPS IN QUALIFYING!

CHILE	VENEZUELA	BOLIVIA	COLOMBIA	ECUADOR	BRAZIL	PARAGUAY	PERU	URUGUAY
Drew 2-2 (h)	Won 3-0 (a)	Won 3-0 (h)	Drew 1-1 (a)	Won 1-0 (a)	Lost 3-1 (a)	Drew 0-0 (h)	Won 3-1 (a)	Won 4-2 (h)
Cavallero	Cavallero	Cavallero	Cavallero	Cavallero	Cavallero	Abbondancieri	Abbondancieri	Abbondancieri
Zanetti	Zanetti	Zanetti	Zanetti	Rodriguez	Zanetti	Sorin	Zanetti	Zanetti
Vivas	Vivas	Quiroga	Quiroga	Sorin	Quiroga	Ayala	Gabriel Milito	Samuel
Ayala	Ayala	Ayala	Ayala	Ayala	Heinze	Samuel	Coloccini 1	Heinze
Samuel	Placente	Samuel	Samuel	Heinze	Sorin 1	Heinze	Heinze	Coloccini
Veron	Veron	Almeyda	Placente	Luis Gonzalez	Samuel	Mascherano	Mascherano	Sorin
D'Alessandro	D'Alessandro	D'Alessandro 1	Almeyda	Aimar	Mascherano	Luis Gonzalez	Rosales 1	Cambiasso
Aimar 1	Aimar 1	Aimar 1	Aimar	D'Alessandro	Luis Gonzalez	Kily Gonzalez	D'Alessandro	Riquelme
Kily Gonzalez 1	Kily Gonzalez	Kily Gonzalez	Kily Gonzalez	Kily Gonzalez	Kily Gonzalez	Tevez	Tevez	Saviola
Delgado	Delgado 1	Delgado	Delgado	Delgado	Delgado	Saviola	Kily Gonzalez	Luis Gonzalez 1
Crespo	Crespo 1	Crespo 1	Crespo 1	Crespo 1	Crespo	Crespo	Delgado	Figueroa 2
Substitutes:	**Substitutes:**	**Substitutes:**	**Substitutes:**	**Substitutes:**	**Substitutes:**	**Substitutes:**	**Substitutes:**	**Substitutes:**
Almeyda 69	Heinze 63	Saviola 80	Veron 46	Tevez 46	Rosales 36	Rosales 66	Diego Milito 63	Maxi Rodriguez
Saviola 72	Almeyda 81	Sorin 84	Saviola 70	Riquelme 56	Aimar 61		Sorin 1 69	Insua
	Luis Gonzalez 85	Cambiasso 89	D'Alessandro 71	Burdisso 65	Saviola 61		Medina 83	

| MOST GOALS! | HERNAN CRESPO 28 | WORLD RANKING! | 4TH | WORLD CUP ODDS! | 7/1 | WORLD CUP BEST! | WINNERS 1978, 1986 |

⭐ ROAD TO THE FINALS! ⭐

South America	P	W	D	L	F	A	Pts
Brazil	18	9	7	2	35	17	34
Argentina	18	10	4	4	29	17	34
Ecuador	18	8	4	6	23	19	28
Paraguay	18	8	4	6	23	23	28
Uruguay	18	6	7	5	23	28	25
Colombia	18	6	6	6	24	16	24
Chile	18	5	7	6	18	22	22
Venezuela	18	5	3	10	20	28	18
Peru	18	4	6	8	20	28	18
Bolivia	18	4	2	12	20	37	14

TOP SCORER

| Hernan Crespo | 7 |

Juan Riquelme.

⭐ PLAYER TO WATCH! ⭐

Esteban Cambiasso
Quitting Real Madrid was a smart move for Cambiasso, because he's now a key player for Inter Milan and for Argentina. In a team full of flair players, Cambiasso adds steel and simple passing to the midfield.

⭐ STRONGEST STARTING LINE-UP! 4-2-3-1 ⭐

ABBONDANZIERI

ZANETTI — SAMUEL — HEINZE — SORIN

CAMBIASSO — MASCHERANO

MESSI — SAVIOLA — RIQUELME

CRESPO

⭐ PLAYER TO WATCH! ⭐

Hernan Crespo
Crespo is Argentina's No.1 striker and with all the classy midfielders playing around him, he gets plenty of goalscoring chances! The Chelsea hero was the team's leading scorer in qualifying with seven goals.

⭐ THE PLAYERS! ⭐

GOALKEEPERS
Roberto Abbondanzieri	Boca Juniors
Leonard Franco	Atletico Madrid
German Lux	River Plate

DEFENDERS
Roberto Ayala	Valencia
Nicolas Burdisso	Inter Milan
Fabricio Coloccini	Deportivo
Gabriel Heinze	Man. United
Gabriel Milito	Real Zaragoza
Gonzalo Rodriguez	Villarreal
Walter Samuel	Inter Milan
Juan Pablo Sorin	Villarreal
Javier Zanetti	Inter Milan

MIDFIELDERS
Pablo Aimar	Valencia
Sebastian Battaglia	Boca Juniors
Esteban Cambiasso	Inter Milan
Martin Demichelis	Bayern Munich
Kily Gonzalez	Inter Milan
Luis Gonzalez	Porto
Javier Mascherano	Corinthians
Lionel Messi	Barcelona
Juan Riquelme	Villarreal
Carlos Tevez	Corinthians

STRIKERS
Hernan Crespo	Chelsea
Julio Cruz	Inter Milan
Cesar Delgado	Cruz Azul
Luciano Figueroa	Villarreal
Diego Milito	Real Zaragoza
Javier Saviola	Seville

Lionel Messi.

⭐ RESULTS AND LINE-UPS IN QUALIFYING! ⭐

CHILE	VENEZUELA	BOLIVIA	COLOMBIA	ECUADOR	BRAZIL	PARAGUAY	PERU	URUGUAY
Drew 0-0 (a)	Won 3-2* (h)	Won 2-1 (a)	Won 1-0 (h)	Lost 2-0 (a)	Won 3-1 (h)	Lost 1-0 (a)	Won 2-0* (h)	Lost 1-0 (a)
...ondancieri	Abbondancieri	Abbondancieri	Abbondancieri	Franco	Abbondancieri	Abbondancieri	Abbondancieri	Abbondancieri
...etti	Zanetti	Gonzalo Rodriguez	Zanetti	Zanetti	Ayala	Ayala	Ayala	Ayala
...nuel	Gonzalo Rodriguez	Gabriel Milito	Ayala	Coloccini	Coloccini	Coloccini	Coloccini	Samuel
...ze	Gabriel Milito	Burdisso	Heinze	Gabriel Milito	Heinze	Heinze	Gabriel Milito	Ponzio
...occini	Sorin	Cufre	Sorin	Samuel	Sorin	Sorin	Sorin	Sorin
...in	Mascherano	Scaloni	Mascherano	Duscher	Mascherano	Zabaleta	Battaglia	Battaglia
...mbiasso	Cambiasso	Duscher	Cambiasso	Galletti	Riquelme 1	Cambiasso	Riquelme 1	Riquelme
...uelme	Riquelme 1	Cambiasso	Riquelme	Cambiasso	Luis Gonzalez	Riquelme	Luis Gonzalez	Luis Gonzalez
...ola	Solari	Galletti 1	Saviola	Aimar	Kily Gonzalez	Farias	Messi	Kily Gonzalez
...s Gonzalez	Delgado	Maxi Rodriguez	Luis Gonzalez	Kily Gonzalez	Saviola	Luis Gonzalez	Messi	Tevez
...eroa	Figueroa	Figueroa 1	Crespo 1	Maxi Rodriguez	Crespo 2	Delgado	Crespo	Crespo
Substitutes:	**Substitutes:**	**Substitutes:**	**Substitutes:**	**Substitutes:**	**Substitutes:**	**Substitutes:**	**Substitutes:**	**Substitutes:**
...scherano 46	Saviola 1 56	Ponzio 63	Galletti 54	Tevez 31	Zanetti 71	D'Alessandro 71	Tevez 58	Delgado 65
...ez 62	Luis Gonzalez 65	Zarate 75	Placente 79	Figueroa 68	Tevez 82	Santana 79	Messi 65	Messi 65
...essandro 76	Placente 79	Palacio 84		D'Alessandro 74	Messi 80			Aimar 80

HOLLAND!

COACH!	MARCO VAN BASTEN	WORLD RANKING!	3RD	WORLD CUP ODDS!	12/1	WORLD CUP BEST!	RUNNERS-UP 1974, 1978

Ruud van Nistelrooy.

ROAD TO THE FINALS!

Group 1 Europe	P	W	D	L	F	A	Pts
Holland	12	10	2	0	27	3	32
Czech Republic	12	9	0	3	35	12	27
Romania	12	8	1	3	20	10	25
Finland	12	5	1	6	21	19	16
Macedonia	12	2	3	7	11	24	9
Armenia	12	2	1	9	9	25	7
Andorra	12	1	2	9	4	34	5

RESULT	SCORE	OPPOSITION	H/A
Won	2-0	Czech Republic	H
Drew	2-2	Macedonia	A
Won	3-1	Finland	H
Won	3-0	Andorra	A
Won	2-0	Romania	A
Won	2-0	Armenia	H
Won	2-0	Romania	H
Won	4-0	Finland	A
Won	1-0	Armenia	A
Won	4-0	Andorra	H
Won	2-0	Czech Republic	A
Drew	0-0	Macedonia	H

TOP SCORER

Ruud van Nistelrooy	7

Edgar Davids.

THE PLAYERS!

GOALKEEPERS	
Oscar Moens	Willem II
Henk Timmer	AZ Alkmaar
Edwin van der Sar	Man. United

DEFENDERS	
Khalid Boulahrouz	Hamburg
Wilfred Bouma	Aston Villa
Tim de Cler	AZ Alkmaar
Nigel de Jong	Hamburg
Jan Kromkamp	Liverpool
Andre Ooijer	PSV
Barry Opdam	AZ Alkmaar
Giovanni van Bronckhorst	Barcelona
Ron Vlaar	Feyenoord

MIDFIELDERS	
George Boateng	Middlesbrough
Marc van Bommel	Barcelona
Romeo Castelen	Feyenoord
Phillip Cocu	PSV
Edgar Davids	Tottenham
Denny Landzaat	AZ Alkmaar
Olaf Lindenburgh	Ajax
Hedwiges Maduro	Ajax
Wesley Sneijder	Ajax
Rafael van der Vaart	Hamburg

STRIKERS	
Ryan Babel	Ajax
Dirk Kuyt	Feyenoord
Roy Makaay	Bayern Munich
Arjen Robben	Chelsea
Ruud van Nistelrooy	Man. United
Robin van Persie	Arsenal
Jan Vennegor of Hesselink	PSV

STRONGEST STARTING LINE-UP! 4-3-3

VAN DER SAR

KROMKAMP — BOULAHROUZ — OPDAM — VAN BRONCKHORST

LANDZAAT — COCU — VAN DER VAART

KUYT — VAN NISTELROOY — ROBBEN

TEAMTALK!

Euro 2004 was only two years ago, but much of the Holland squad which will go to this World Cup will have changed from back then. Since Marco van Basten became coach, the Dutch have moved out several old stars so they can bring in a group of wicked youngsters. The big change worked, because Holland cruised through their qualifiers, winning eight games and letting in only three goals. Players like Khalid Boulahrouz, Barry Opdam and Denny Landzaat have become big stars and the Dutch are rocking!

MATCHMAN'S VERDICT: "AFTER MISSING OUT ON THE 2002 WORLD CUP FINALS, DA DEADLY DUTCHIES ARE DESPERATE TO MAKE AN IMPACT IN 2006!"

PLAYER TO WATCH!

Arjen Robben

Robben's superb skills are no longer a secret weapon for the Dutch, but that doesn't make him any easier to stop! The 22-year-old has pace, fearsome dribbling skills and a cool finish, and he gives Holland a big attacking edge!

WORLD CUP FINALS 2006

IVORY COAST!

COACH!	HENRI MICHEL	WORLD RANKING!	42ND	WORLD CUP ODDS!	100/1	WORLD CUP BEST!	DEBUT IN FINALS

★ STRONGEST STARTING LINE-UP! 4-4-2

TIZIE

EBOUE — KOLO TOURE — DOMORAUD — BOKA

AKALE — ZOKORA — YAPI — FAE

DROGBA — DINDANE

★ ROAD TO THE FINALS! ★

Group 3 Africa	P	W	D	L	F	A	Pts
Ivory Coast	10	7	1	2	20	7	22
Cameroon	10	6	3	1	18	10	21
Egypt	10	5	2	3	26	15	17
Libya	10	3	3	4	8	10	12
Sudan	10	1	3	6	6	22	6
Benin	10	1	2	7	9	23	5

RESULT	SCORE	OPPOSITION	H/A
Won	2-0	Libya	H
Won	2-1	Egypt	A
Lost	2-0	Cameroon	A
Won	5-0	Sudan	H
Won	1-0	Benin	A
Won	3-0	Benin	H
Drew	0-0	Libya	A
Won	2-0	Egypt	H
Lost	3-2	Cameroon	H
Won	3-1	Sudan	A

TOP SCORERS	
Didier Drogba	9
Aruna Dindane	6

★ TEAMTALK!

Ivory Coast are called 'The Elephants' – and they are on the charge! The Africans secured their first-ever place at the World Cup finals by topping their qualifying group, despite losing twice to Cameroon. The test for these newcomers is a tough one, though. Led by Chelsea striker Didier Drogba and inspired by big players like Kolo Toure, Didier Zokora and Emmanuel Eboue, they do have experience in the team, but Group C is a difficult one and reaching the second round will be another massive achievement!

MATCHMAN'S VERDICT: "GROUP C IS TOUGH FOR ME IVORY COAST BUDS, BUT WATCH 'EM DO THEIR BEST AGAINST DA BIG BOYS!"

★ PLAYER TO WATCH!

Aruna Dindane
Didier Drogba gets the attention as Ivory Coast's main man, but Dindane got plenty of credit after an impressive qualification campaign. The powerful striker scored six goals and carved out plenty of assists for his pal Drogba.

Didier Drogba.

SERBIA-MONTENEGRO!

COACH!	ILIJA PETKOVIC	WORLD RANKING!	47TH	WORLD CUP ODDS!	125/1	WORLD CUP BEST!	SEMI-FINALS 1930

★ STRONGEST STARTING LINE-UP! 4-4-2

JEVRIC

DRAGUTINOVIC — VIDIC — KRSTAJIC — GAVRANCIC

ILIC — VUKIC — STANKOVIC — DJORDJEVIC

KEZMAN — VUCINIC

★ ROAD TO THE FINALS! ★

Group 7 Europe	P	W	D	L	F	A	Pts
Serbia-Mont.	10	6	4	0	16	1	22
Spain	10	5	5	0	19	3	20
Bosnia-Herzeg.	10	4	4	2	12	9	16
Belgium	10	3	3	4	16	11	12
Lithuania	10	2	4	4	8	9	10
San Marino	10	0	0	10	2	40	0

RESULT	SCORE	OPPOSITION	H/A
Won	3-0	San Marino	A
Drew	0-0	Bosnia-Herzegovina	A
Won	5-0	San Marino	H
Won	2-0	Belgium	A
Drew	0-0	Spain	H
Drew	0-0	Belgium	H
Won	2-0	Lithuania	H
Drew	1-1	Spain	A
Won	2-0	Lithuania	A
Won	1-0	Bosnia-Herzegovina	H

TOP SCORERS	
Mateja Kezman	5
Zvonimir Vukic	4

★ TEAMTALK!

Serbia-Montenegro beat Spain to top spot in their group, and boasted an unbeaten record too! Their mega tough defence let in just one goal in ten games, and that was away to Spain! This defensive organisation will be key to the team's chances of getting out of one of the hardest groups in the tournament, and if they keep clean sheets, players like Mateja Kezman and Mirko Vucinic can nick goals for them. They don't have any superstars, but Serbia-Montenegro will be tough to crack in Germany!

MATCHMAN'S VERDICT: "DIS DEFENCE IS TOUGHER THAN A BRICK WALL! THEY AIN'T A TOP TEAM, BUT SERBIA-MONTENEGRO WILL BE DIFFICULT TO BEAT!"

★ PLAYER TO WATCH!

Mirko Vucinic
The 22-year-old has a fine goalscoring reputation after slamming them in for Lecce in the 2004-05 season. Vucinic partners former Chelsea striker Mateja Kezman in attack and his lethal right foot can belt in spectacular goals!

Mateja Kezman.

MATCHY TRANSLATOR!
Need help with your German? MATCHY knows his stuff!

WHAT A GOAL!

YAR! VOT A VUNDERBAR GOL!

WHO'S THIS OLD CHA...

This fuzzy-haired German i... Franz Beckenbauer, the firs... person to win the World Cu... as a captain AND manager

WORLD CUP SHORTIES!

THERE'S GONNA BE SOME WELL SMALL PLAYERS RUNNING AROUND IN GERMANY! CHECK OUT THE MINI DUDES!

WHO

MOHAMMAD AL SHALHOUB SAUDI ARABIA!
5FT 3INS

SHAUN WRIGHT-PHILLIPS ENGLAND!
5FT 5INS

LIONEL MESSI ARGENTINA!
5FT 5INS

ROBINHO BRAZIL!
5FT 6INS

PETER CROUCH ENGLAND!
6FT 7INS

CROUCH AIN'T NO MIDGET - HE'S A GIANT!

LUKAS PODOLSKI

SAMUEL ETO'O:
MY GUIDE TO THE WORLD CUP!

Barcelona striker Sammy Eto'o is well jealous, coz loads of his team-mates are in Germany! But as his country Cameroon did not qualify, MATCH wondered who he thinks will win the cup...

I'm not going, so I don't care who wins it! Laters!

FACT PACK!

Name: Lukas Podolski
Age: 21
Country: Germany
Club: Cologne
Position: Striker
Top skill: Clinical finishing!
Transfer value: £8 million

WHAT BOOTS DOES...

Brazil's Ronaldo wear? **Nike Mercurial Vapor III**

IS IT A GIRL?

Check out the dodgy haircuts of these World Cup stars!

FRANCESCO TOTTI ITALY

GUTI SPAIN

HERNAN CRESPO ARGENTINA

THE HELL IS...

MATCH reveals three players who could become big stars at the 2006 World Cup!

I'M GONNA ROCK!

'Prince Poldi' is a big hit with the fans after grabbing ten goals in his first 17 games for Germany!

DIDIER ZOKORA!

FACT PACK!

Name: Carlos Tevez

Age: 22

Country: Argentina

Club: Corinthians

Position: Midfield/striker

Top skill: Flashy feet!

Transfer value: £15 million

CARLOS TEVEZ!

I LOVE AWARDS, ME!

FACT PACK!

Name: Didier Zokora

Age: 25

Country: Ivory Coast

Club: St. Etienne

Position: Midfield

Top skill: Crunching tackles!

Transfer value: £10 million

'El Maestro' is big mates with Chelsea striker Didier Drogba and Arsenal defender Kolo Toure!

'El Apache' has been voted South America's best footballer for the last three years! Come to the Prem!

MEXICO!

| COACH! | RICARDO LA VOLPE | CAPTAIN! | RAFAEL MARQUEZ | MOST CAPS! | PAVEL PARDO 112 |

⭐ QUALIFYING FORM! ⭐

An easy play-off with Dominica and a first group with Trinidad & Tobago, St Kitts & Nevis and St Vincent, Mexico came second behind USA to make the finals. They finished top scorers in the group with 22 goals, only dropping points in a 1-1 draw with Panama and defeats to USA and Trinidad & Tobago!

⭐ STRENGTHS! ⭐

Mexico have a top 'keeper in Oswaldo Sanchez, who's in the form of his life. Their defence is one of the best too, so Mexico are a hard team to beat. They also have loads of attacking threat in midfield – Jaime Lozano netted 11 times in qualifying!

⭐ WEAKNESSES! ⭐

Mexico scored goals for fun on their way to the finals, but they won't be facing such easy teams now. They may find the step up in class and competition a massive shock when the World Cup kicks off!

Zinha.

⭐ CAN THEY WIN? ⭐

In a word, no! Mexico are ranked joint seventh in the world, ahead of England, but that's more to do with the teams they play in qualifying are rubbish, so they pick up loads of easy wins. A solid defence is a wicked thing to have, but it will only get you so far and up against Brazil, Argentina or one of the top European teams, it won't be easy!

MATCHMAN'S VERDICT: "ARRRIBA! MEXICO WERE ON FIRE QUALIFYIN' FOR DA WORLD CUP FINALS, BUT THEY'LL FIND IT TOUGHER IN DA REAL THING. LAST EIGHT AT BEST!"

⭐ RESULTS AND LINE-UPS IN QUALIFYING!

DOMINICA	DOMINICA	TRINIDAD & TOB.	ST. VIN/GREN	ST. VIN/GREN	TRINIDAD & TOB.	ST. KITTS/NEVIS	ST. KITTS/NEVIS	COSTA RICA
Won 10-0 (a)	Won 8-0 (h)	Won 3-1 (a)	Won 7-0 (h)	Won 1-0 (a)	Won 3-0 (a)	Won 5-0 (a)	Won 8-0 (h)	Won 2-1 (a)
Sanchez 0	Perez	Sanchez 0	Sanchez 0	Sanchez 0	Sanchez 0	Munoz	Munoz	Perez 0
Osorio	Osorio	Rodriguez F	Rodriguez F	Rodriguez F	Rodriguez F	Rodriguez F	Rodriguez F	Carmona
Davino 1	Davino	Carmona	Lopez	Lopez	Mendez	Galindo	Rodriguez JP	Sanchez H
Marquez 1	Marquez	Salcido	Marquez	Marquez	Salcido	Rodriguez JP	Sanchez H	Marquez
Palencia 1	Osorno	Sanchez H	Salcido	Salcido	Sanchez H	Olalde	Olalde	Salcido
Pardo	Pardo	Pardo	Zinha	Zinha	Zinha 1	Altamirano 1	Garcia	Pardo
Altamirano	Altamirano 1	Perez M	Mendez	Mendez	Garcia	Perez M	Pirez L 3	Zinha
Valdez	Lozano 2	Zinha	Lozano 2	Lozano	Lozano 2	Garcia	Garcia	Lozano 2
Torrado	Torrado	Perez L	Blanco	Blanco	Borgetti	Pineda	Pineda	Blanco
Borgetti 2	Borgetti 2	Borgetti 1	Borgetti 4	Borgetti 1	Arellano	Fonseca 2	Altamirano 1	Borgetti
Bautista 2	Bautista 2	Arellano 2	Arellano	Arellano		Santana 2	Fonseca 2	Fonseca
Substitutes:	**Substitutes:**	**Substitutes:**	**Substitutes:**	**Substitutes:**	**Substitutes:**	**Substitutes:**	**Substitutes:**	
Osorno 1 46	Oteo 1 46	Pineda 74	Garcia 66	Sanchez H 18	Arce 81	Medina 64	Osorno 1 31	Altamirano
Lozano 2 62	Morales 60	Altamirano 84	Perez 66	Osorno 64	Pineda 83	Osorno 66	Medina 46	Medina
Arellano 62	Palencia 71		Santana 1 72	Perez L 78	Santana 84	Valdez 78	Santana 1 58	Pineda

MOST GOALS!	JARED BORGETTI 37	WORLD RANKING!	14TH	WORLD CUP ODDS!	40/1	WORLD CUP BEST!	QUARTER-FINALS 1970, 1986

⭐ PLAYER TO WATCH! ⭐
Rafael Marquez
Marquez is the man! The Barcelona stopper is the type of guy you want in defence – he's aggressive, reads the game well and is strong in the air. Mexico's skipper can also play as a holding midfielder!

⭐ ROAD TO THE FINALS! ⭐

Stage 2 Group 3	P	W	D	L	F	A	Pts
Mexico	6	6	0	0	27	1	18
Trinidad & Tobago	6	4	0	2	12	9	12
St Vincent/Gren.	6	2	0	4	5	12	6
St Kitts & St Nevis	6	0	0	6	2	24	0

Stage 3	P	W	D	L	F	A	Pts
USA	10	7	1	2	16	6	22
Mexico	10	7	1	2	22	9	22
Costa Rica	10	5	1	4	15	14	16
Trinidad & Tobago	10	4	1	5	10	15	13
Guatemala	10	3	2	5	16	18	11
Panama	10	0	2	8	4	21	2

TOP SCORERS

Jared Borgetti	14
Jaime Lozano	11
Jose Fonseca	10

Ricardo Osorio.

⭐ THE PLAYERS! ⭐

GOALKEEPERS
Jose Corona	Tecos UAG
Moises Munoz	Monarcas Morelia
Oswaldo Sanchez	Chivas Guadalajara

DEFENDERS
Salvador Carmona	Cruz Azul
Duilio Davino	Club America
Aaron Galindo	Cruz Azul
Joel Huiqui	Cruz Azul
Rafael Marquez	Barcelona
Mario Mendez	Toluca
Ramon Morales	Chivas Guadalajara
Ricardo Osorio	Cruz Azul
Pavel Pardo	Club America
Gonzalo Pineda	Pumas UNAM
Francisco Rodriguez	Chivas Guadalajara
Carlos Salcido	Chivas Guadalajara
Hugo Sanchez	Tigres

MIDFIELDERS
Hector Altamirano	San Luis
Gerardo Galindo	Pumas UNAM
Rafael Garcia	Toluca
Jaime Lozano	Pumas UNAM
Alberto Medina	Chivas Guadalajara
Luis Perez	Monterrey
Juan Pablo Rodriguez	Chivas Guadalajar
Gerardo Torrado	Cruz Azul
Zinha	Toluca

STRIKERS
Jesus Arellano	Monterrey
Cuauhtemoc Blanco	Club America
Jared Borgetti	Bolton
Omar Bravo	Chivas Guadalajara
Jose Fonseca	Cruz Azul

⭐ STRONGEST STARTING LINE-UP! 4-4-2 ⭐

SANCHEZ

OSORIO — MARQUEZ — SALCIDO — RODRIGUEZ F

PARDO — ZINHA — LOZANO — PEREZ L

FONSECA — BORGETTI

⭐ PLAYER TO WATCH! ⭐
Jared Borgetti
Borgetti struggled a bit for Bolton last season, but for Mexico he's a goalscoring king! The big striker was the highest scorer across the world in the qualifying stages, banging in 14 goals in 14 games!

Jose Fonseca.

⭐ RESULTS AND LINE-UPS IN QUALIFYING! ⭐

USA	PANAMA	GUATEMALA	TRINIDAD & TOB.	COSTA RICA	USA	PANAMA	GUATEMALA	TRINIDAD & TOB.
Won 2-1 (h)	Drew 1-1 (a)	Won 2-0* (a)	Won 2-0 (h)	Won 2-0 (h)	Lost 2-0 (a)	Won 5-0 (h)	Won 5-2 (h)	Lost 2-1 (a)
Sanchez 0	Sanchez 0	Sanchez 0	Sanchez 0	Sanchez 0	Sanchez 0	Sanchez 0	Corona 0	Corona
Osorio	Osorio	Osorio	Osorio	Osorio	Davino	Rodriguez F	Osorio	Rodriguez F
Carmona	Carmona	Carmona	Mendez	Rodriguez F	Rodriguez F	Pineda	Rodriguez F	Lopez I
Marquez	Marquez	Marquez	Rodriguez J	Marquez	Marquez	Marquez 1	Lopez I	Huiqui
Salcido	Salcido	Salcido	Salcido	Salcido	Salcido	Pineda	Pineda	Sanchez H
Pardo	Rodriguez J	Galindo	Galindo	Pardo	Galindo	Pardo 1	Torrado	Morales
Morales 1	Zinha 1	Zinha	Zinha	Galindo	Zinha	Zinha	Lozano	Lozano 1
Altamirano	Lozano	Lozano	Zinha	Morales	Morales	Morales	Mendez	Rojas
Perez L	Perez L 1	Perez L 1	Torrado	Torrado	Perez L 1	Perez L	Perez L
Borgetti 1	Borgetti	Borgetti 1	Borgetti 1	Borgetti	Borgetti 1	Franco 1	Fonseca
Blanco	Fonseca	Fonseca	Fonseca 1	Fonseca	Rojas	Fonseca 4	Franco

Substitutes:	Substitutes:	Substitutes:	Substitutes:	Substitutes:	Substitutes:	Substitutes:	Substitutes:	Substitutes:
Medina 65	Pineda 56	Pineda 68	Medina 36	Morales 46	Medina 58	Medina 45	Rojas 55	Briseno 46
Morales 69	Garcia 58	Galindo 72	Morales 62	Pineda 60	Mendez 59	Morales C 69	Huiqui 58	Mendez M 67
Perez L 69	Medina 70	Bravo 74	Bravo 84	Bravo 67	Bravo 69	Fonseca 1 71	Morales C	Rodriguez JP 74

PORTUGAL!

| COACH! | LUIZ FELIPE SCOLARI | WORLD RANKING! | 10TH | WORLD CUP ODDS! | 18/1 | WORLD CUP BEST! | SEMI-FINALS 1966 |

Cristiano Ronaldo.

★ ROAD TO THE FINALS! ★

Group 3 Europe	P	W	D	L	F	A	Pts
Portugal	12	9	3	0	35	5	30
Slovakia	12	6	5	1	24	8	23
Russia	12	6	5	1	23	12	23
Estonia	12	5	2	5	16	17	17
Latvia	12	4	3	5	18	21	15
Liechtenstein	12	2	2	8	13	23	8
Luxembourg	12	0	0	12	5	48	0

RESULT	SCORE	OPPOSITION	H/A
Won	2-0	Latvia	A
Won	4-0	Estonia	H
Drew	2-2	Liechtenstein	A
Won	7-1	Russia	H
Won	5-0	Luxembourg	A
Drew	1-1	Slovakia	A
Won	2-0	Slovakia	H
Won	1-0	Estonia	A
Won	6-0	Luxembourg	H
Drew	0-0	Russia	A
Won	2-1	Liechtenstein	H
Won	3-0	Latvia	H

TOP SCORERS

Pauleta	11
Cristiano Ronaldo	7

Luis Figo.

★ STRONGEST STARTING LINE-UP! 4-4-1-1 ★

RICARDO

FERREIRA — CARVALHO — ANDRADE — VALENTE

RONALDO — MANICHE — COSTINHA — SIMAO

DECO

PAULETA

★ TEAMTALK! ★

If their qualifying campaign was anything to go by, Portugal will be confident of having a storming World Cup this summer. They won the group easily, finishing unbeaten and seven points ahead of Slovakia. Plus, they whupped Russia 7-1 and Pauleta was the top scorer in European qualifying with 11 goals. Portugal have loads of attacking talent with Ronaldo, Figo, Maniche, Deco and Simao in the squad, and will hope to do better than the last World Cup where they crashed out in the first round!

MATCHMAN SAYS: "THESE PORTU-GEEZERS 'AVE GOT SKILL AND ARE IN AN EASY GROUP. I RECKS THEY IS GONNA GO A LONG WAY IN GERMANY!"

★ PLAYER TO WATCH! ★

Pauleta

After poor performances at Euro 2004, Pauleta answered his critics by scoring 11 goals in qualifying – the best of any player in Europe. At 33, this will be his last World Cup and his cool penalty box finishing will be vital for Portugal!

★ THE PLAYERS! ★

GOALKEEPERS

Ricardo	Sporting Lisbon
Quim	Benfica

DEFENDERS

Jorge Andrade	Deportivo
Marco Caneira	Valencia
Ricardo Carvalho	Chelsea
Paulo Ferreira	Chelsea
Fernando Meira	Stuttgart
Miguel Monteiro	Benfica
Jorge Ribeiro	Gil Vicente
Nuno Valente	Everton

MIDFIELDERS

Luis Boa Morte	Fulham
Costinha	Porto
Deco	Barcelona
Luis Figo	Inter Milan
Maniche	Dynamo
Joao Moutinho	Sporting Lisbon
Armando Petit	Benfica
Ricardo Quaresma	Porto
Cristiano Ronaldo	Man. United
Simao Sabrosa	Benfica
Tiago	Lyon
Hugo Viana	Newcastle

STRIKERS

Hugo Almeida	Porto
Ricardo Costa	Porto
Nuno Gomes	Benfica
Pauleta	PSG
Helder Postiga	Porto

IRAN!

| COACH! | BRANKO IVANKOVIC | WORLD RANKING! | 19TH | WORLD CUP ODDS! | 500/1 | WORLD CUP BEST! | FIRST ROUND 1978, 1998, 2002 |

★ STRONGEST STARTING LINE-UP! 4-4-2 ★

MIRZAPOUR

GOLMOHAMMADI — KABEI — REZAEI — NOSRATI

KARIMI — NEKOUNAM — MAHDAVIKIA — ZANDI

HASHEMIAN — DAEI

★ ROAD TO THE FINALS! ★

Asia Gp2 Stage 3	P	W	D	L	F	A	Pts
Japan	6	5	0	1	9	4	15
Iran	6	4	1	1	7	3	13
Bahrain	6	1	1	4	4	7	4
North Korea	6	1	0	5	5	11	3

RESULT	SCORE	OPPOSITION	H/A
Drew	0-0	Bahrain	A
Won	2-1	Japan	H
Won	2-0	North Korea	H
Won	1-0	North Korea	H
Won	1-0	Bahrain	H
Lost	2-1	Japan	A

TOP SCORERS	
Ali Daei	9
Vahid Hashemian	4

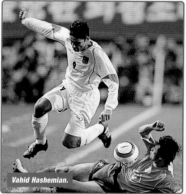

Vahid Hashemian.

★ TEAMTALK! ★

Iran have never been great at the World Cup – the team didn't get past the group stages in three previous attempts – but hopes are high this time around. The current squad is probably the best Iran have ever had, though veteran striker Ali Daei is still expected to score most of the goals. Daei will be joined in attack by Vahid Hashemian, who was persuaded out of international retirement during the qualifiers. If these two get their scoring boots on, then Iran have a chance of making the second stage.

MATCHMAN SAYS: "IRAN 'AVE A LEGEND IN ALI DAEI WHO SCORES GOALS FOR FUN, BUT I DON'T RECKS THEY'LL BEAT MEXICO AND PORTUGAL!"

★ PLAYER TO WATCH! ★

Ali Daei

The 37-year-old striker is a true footy legend in Iran! Daei has clocked up an amazing 107 goals for Iran, which is more than any other international striker in history, and he'll be out for a few more this summer!

ANGOLA!

| COACH! | LUIS OLIVEIRA GONCALVES | WORLD RANKING! | 62ND | WORLD CUP ODDS! | 400/1 | WORLD CUP BEST! | DEBUT IN FINALS |

★ STRONGEST STARTING LINE-UP! 4-4-2 ★

JOAO PERREIRA

JACINTO — JAMBA — LEBO LEBO — YAMBA ASHA

FLAVIO — FIGUEIREDO — ANDRE — GILBERTO

MANTORRAS — AKWA

★ ROAD TO THE FINALS! ★

Africa Group 1	P	W	D	L	F	A	Pts
Angola	10	6	3	1	12	6	21
Nigeria	10	6	3	1	21	7	21
Zimbabwe	10	4	3	3	13	14	15
Gabon	10	2	4	4	11	13	10
Algeria	10	1	5	4	8	15	8
Rwanda	10	1	2	7	6	16	5

RESULT	SCORE	OPPOSITION	H/A
Lost	3-1	Chad (qualifier)	A
Won	2-0	Chad (qualifier)	H
Drew	0-0	Algeria	A
Won	1-0	Nigeria	H
Drew	2-2	Gabon	A
Won	1-0	Rwanda	H
Won	1-0	Zimbabwe	H
Lost	2-0	Zimbabwe	A
Won	2-1	Algeria	H
Drew	1-1	Nigeria	A
Won	3-0	Gabon	H
Won	1-0	Rwanda	A

TOP SCORERS	
Akwa	5
Bruno Mauro	2
Flavio	2

Flavio.

★ TEAMTALK! ★

Angola nearly went out in the early qualifying stages before coming back to beat little Chad on away goals! They then found their best form to top a strong qualifying group that included Nigeria and Zimbabwe. Angola are a tough defensive side who try to be hard to beat, but they've got plenty of pace up front too with Akwa leading their attack. Coach Luis Oliveira Goncalves is already a star in Angola, but if he gets them through this group, he'll be a living legend in the country!

MATCHMAN'S VERDICT: "ANGOLA STORMED TO DA FINALS, BUT STAR STRIKER AKWA NEEDS TO WORK SOME MAGIC TO GET 'EM OUTTA THIS GROUP!"

★ PLAYER TO WATCH! ★

Akwa

Akwa is a top player who knows where the goal is! The striker is also Angola's captain and his country's all-time top goalscorer and most capped footballer, with 31 strikes from 68 games. Watch out for him in Germany!

PLANET FOOTY!

WORLD CUP LOOPY!
THE FOOTY HAS SENT THIS FAN BONKERS!

GO CRAZE GO-AL

ER, WHO TURNED OUT THE LIGHTS?

SHAKE IT BABY, SHAKE IT!

INVISIBLE DJ!

LUCA TONI
ITALY
What happens? The striker covers his ear as if he's wearing headphones and spins an invisible disc with his other hand. Rockin'!

PARTY RATING:

I'VE SEEN THAT! ✓

THE SCREAMING FLYER!

FERNANDO TORRES
SPAIN
What happens? He sticks his arms out like a plane, and flies towards the crowd with his eyes shut and roaring loud!

PARTY RATING:

I'VE SEEN THAT! ✓

THE WRIST TWIST!

RONALDINHO
BRAZIL
What happens? Ronnie sticks his thumb and little finger out, and runs away smiling and spinning his wrists! Party time!

PARTY RATING:

I'VE SEEN THAT! ✓

CLASSIC CELEBRATIONS!

THE SKY POINTER!

GARY LINEKER
ENGLAND
MEXICO '86

THE BOOTY SHAKE!

ROGER MILLA
CAMEROON
ITALY '90

THE CRAZY!

DIEGO MARADONA
ARGENTINA
USA '94

THE SEVEN TIMER!

JULIUS AGHAHOWA
NIGERIA
JAPAN/S. KOREA '02

SHIRT DANCE!

PAPA BOUBA DIOP
SENEGAL
JAPAN/S. KOREA '02

THE BOXERS!

TIM CAHILL & ARCHIE THOMPSON
AUSTRALIA
What happens? The Ozzie nutters leg it to the corner flag and use it to practise their boxing moves!

PARTY RATING:

I'VE SEEN THAT! ✓

LONGEST SERVING MANAGERS!

BRUCE ARENA
USA
SINCE OCTOBER 1998!

LARS LAGERBACK
SWEDEN
SINCE JANUARY 2000!

SVEN GORAN ERIKSSON
ENGLAND
SINCE JANUARY 2001!

KOBI KUHN
SWITZERLAND
SINCE JUNE 2001!

NEW BOY!

DON'T PICK ON THE NEWBY!

MARCOS PAQUETA
SAUDI ARABIA
SINCE DECEMBER 2005!

EEE!

Players go proper nuttso when they score for their country! Here's the MATCH guide to crazy celebrations on show this summer – tick 'em off when ya see them on TV!

BUST SOME MOVES, PUNKS!

THE BODY POP!

RIO FERDINAND
ENGLAND
What happens? If Rio springs a surprise and scores, expect to see him celebrate with a body bustin' robot dance!

PARTY RATING:

I'VE SEEN THAT! ✓

IVORY FLOAT!

DIDIER DROGBA
IVORY COAST
What happens? DD's team-mates chase after him, they form a circle and then jump up and down kicking out their legs!

PARTY RATING:

I'VE SEEN THAT! ✓

THE FLYIN' FLIP!

MIROSLAV KLOSE
GERMANY
What happens? After scoring, he runs away from goal with his arms out wide before pulling off a flying somersault!

PARTY RATING:

I'VE SEEN THAT! ✓

MEGA RIVAL SMACKDOWN!

OVER THE YEARS, SOME MEGA RIVALRIES HAVE KICKED OFF BETWEEN COUNTRIES! IF THIS LOT MEET UP, WATCH OUT!

AUSTRALIA v CROATIA

WHY THE BEEF?
Loads of Croatians live in Oz, and they say Viduka should play for them coz he was born there! They're in Group F!

Er, I'm confused!

WHEN WILL THEY CLASH? GROUP STAGES!

ENGLAND v ARGENTINA

Good evening.

I hate you.

WHY THE BEEF?
Argentina knocked England out of the '86 World Cup when Maradona punched the ball in the net! This clash is tasty!

WHEN COULD THEY CLASH? QUARTER-FINALS!

ITALY v SOUTH KOREA

WHY THE BEEF?
South Korea sent star-studded Italy home from the last World Cup in the second stage! Italy want revenge!

Easy, easy, easy!

Noooo! Not fair!

WHEN COULD THEY CLASH? QUARTER-FINALS!

GHANA v IVORY COAST

We're gonna get ya!

WHY THE BEEF?
The West African rivals have the hopes of their continent on their shoulders – both wanna be the best!

WHEN COULD THEY CLASH? SEMI-FINALS!

ITALY!

COACH!	MARCELLO LIPPI
CAPTAIN!	FABIO CANNAVARO
MOST CAPS!	FABIO CANNAVARO 90

⭐ QUALIFYING FORM! ⭐

Italy cruised through without many hiccups, but also without impressing much! The competition wasn't strong for the Italians, who lost once and wrapped up their qualification with a hard-fought win in Palermo over Slovenia, defender Cristian Zaccardo scoring late on to clinch a 1-0 win.

⭐ STRENGTHS! ⭐

Italy have loads of forward options with Roma ace Francesco Totti, if fit, used in a deeper role behind Alberto Gilardino and Luca Toni. But there's quality back-up too, with Alessandro del Piero, Real Madrid striker Antonio Cassano and Christian Vieri.

⭐ WEAKNESSES! ⭐

The Italians are concerned about their centre-backs. Fabio Cannavaro and Alessandro Nesta are excellent, but if either of these two are injured or suspended – which is what happened back in the 2002 World Cup – Italy could be in big trouble at the back!

Gennaro Gattuso.

⭐ CAN THEY WIN? ⭐

Italy are always one of the strongest teams in tournaments, but their world ranking of 12th shows that recent performances haven't been great. The team was poor in the last World Cup and again at Euro 2004, and they've picked up a nasty habit of losing or drawing games they should win quite easily. If Italy can win the mental battle, they're halfway there!

MATCHMAN'S VERDICT: "YA NEVER KNOW ABOUT ITALY! THEY'VE GOT WELL-WICKED PLAYERS, BUT SOMETIMES THEY JUST FLOP BIG STYLE!"

Gianluigi Buffon.

⭐ RESULTS AND LINE-UPS IN QUALIFYING!

NORWAY	MOLDOVA	SLOVENIA	BELARUS	SCOTLAND	NORWAY
Won 2-1 (h)	Won 1-0 (a)	Lost 1-0 (a)	Won 4-3 (h)	Won 2-0 (h)	Drew 0-0 (a)
Buffon	Buffon	Buffon	Buffon	Buffon	Buffon
Bonera	Bonera	Bonera	Oddo	Bonera	Bonera
Favalli	Zambrotta	Zambrotta	Pancaro	Chiellini	Grosso
Nesta	Nesta	Nesta	Nesta	Cannavaro	Cannavaro
Materazzi	Materazzi	Cannavaro	Materazzi	Materazzi	Materazzi
Fiore	Diana	Camoranesi	Diana	Camoranesi	Camoranesi
De Rossi 1	Pirlo	Gattuso	Gattuso	Pirlo 2	Pirlo
Gattuso	Ambrosini	De Rossi	De Rossi 1	Gattuso	De Rossi
Zambrotta	Gattuso	Esposito	Zambrotta	Totti	Zambrotta
Miccoli	Del Piero 1	Totti	Totti 2	Cassano	Vieri
Gilardino	Gilardino	Gilardino	Gilardino 1	Gilardino	Cassano
Substitutes	**Substitutes**	**Substitutes**	**Substitutes**	**Substitutes**	**Substitutes**
Corradi 59	Oddo 73	Fiore 68	Perrotta 64	De Rossi 70	Toni
Diana 70	Toni 80	Toni 68	Cannavaro 68	Toni 82	Iaquinta
Toni 1 74	Blasi 84	Di Vaio 83	Blasi 74		Diana

WORLD CUP FINALS 2006
GROUP E

MOST GOALS!	DEL PIERO, VIERI 23	WORLD RANKING!	12TH	WORLD CUP ODDS!	11/1	WORLD CUP BEST!	WINNERS 1934, 1938, 1982

★ ROAD TO THE FINALS! ★

Group 5 Europe	P	W	D	L	F	A	Pts
Italy	10	7	2	1	17	8	23
Norway	10	5	3	2	12	7	18
Scotland	10	3	4	3	9	7	13
Slovenia	10	3	3	4	10	13	12
Belarus	10	2	4	4	12	14	10
Moldova	10	1	2	7	5	16	5

TOP SCORER	
Luca Toni	4

Antonio Cassano.

★ PLAYER TO WATCH! ★
Luca Toni
Toni is coming good at the perfect time. Last season he scored loads of goals for Fiorentina and when he banged in a brilliant hat-trick against Belarus, the whole of Italy was gripped by Toni mania!

★ STRONGEST STARTING LINE-UP! 4-3-1-2 ★

BUFFON

ZAMBROTTA CANNAVARO NESTA GROSSO

CAMORANESI PIRLO GATTUSO

TOTTI

GILARDINO TONI

★ PLAYER TO WATCH! ★
Andrea Pirlo
It took Pirlo a while to get a place in Italy's team, but now he's a vital player. The AC Milan midfielder sits just in front of his defence, where he can ping superb passes around. Watch out for his deadly free-kicks!

★ THE PLAYERS! ★

GOALKEEPERS	
Gianluigi Buffon	Juventus
Morgan de Sanctis	Udinese
Angelo Peruzzi	Lazio

DEFENDERS	
Andrea Barzagli	Palermo
Daniele Bonera	Parma
Fabio Cannavaro	Juventus
Fabio Grosso	Palermo
Marco Materazzi	Inter Milan
Alessandro Nesta	AC Milan
Massimo Oddo	Lazio
Cristian Zaccardo	Palermo
Gianluca Zambrotta	Juventus

MIDFIELDERS	
Simone Barone	Palermo
Manuele Blasi	Juventus
Mauro Camoranesi	Juventus
Daniele de Rossi	Roma
Aimo Diana	Sampdoria
Stefano Fiore	Fiorentina
Gennaro Gattuso	AC Milan
Simone Perrotta	Roma
Andrea Pirlo	AC Milan
Francesco Totti	Roma

STRIKERS	
Antonio Cassano	Real Madrid
Alessandro Del Piero	Juventus
Alberto Gilardino	AC Milan
Vincenzo Iaquinta	Udinese
Cristiano Lucarelli	Livorno
Luca Toni	Fiorentina
Christian Vieri	Monaco

Fabio Cannavaro.

Alessandro del Piero.

SCOTLAND	BELARUS	SLOVENIA	MOLDOVA
Drew 1-1 (a)	Won 4-1 (a)	Won 1-0 (h)	Won 2-1 (h)
ruzzi	Peruzzi	Peruzzi	De Sanctis
ccardo	Zaccardo	Zambrotta	Zaccardo
mbrotta	Grosso	Grosso	Grosso
sta	Nesta	Nesta	Bonera
nnavaro	Cannavaro	Cannavaro	Materazzi
	Camoranesi 1	Camoranesi	Diana
ttuso	Pirlo	Pirlo	Barone
Rossi	Gattuso	Gattuso	De Rossi
ti	Totti	Totti	Del Piero
eri	Toni 3	Toni	Vieri 1
quinta	Gilardino	Gilardino	Iaquinta
Substitutes	**Substitutes**	**Substitutes**	**Substitutes**
osso 1 46	Barone 56	Zaccardo 1 60	Blasi 45
moranesi 60	Iaquinta 65	De Rossi 81	Zambrotta 61
i 70	Barzagli 83	Vieri 87	Gilardino 1 67

CZECH REPUBLIC!

COACH!	KAREL BRUCKNER

WORLD RANKING!	2ND

WORLD CUP ODDS!	33/1

WORLD CUP BEST!	RUNNERS-UP 1934, 1962

Rosicky, Nedved & Smicer.

ROAD TO THE FINALS!

Group 1 Europe	P	W	D	L	F	A	Pts
Holland	12	10	2	0	27	3	32
Czech Republic	12	9	0	3	35	12	27
Romania	12	8	1	3	20	10	25
Finland	12	5	1	6	21	19	16
Macedonia	12	2	3	7	11	24	9
Armenia	12	2	1	9	9	25	7
Andorra	12	1	2	9	4	34	5

RESULT	SCORE	OPPOSITION	H/A
Lost	2-0	Holland	A
Won	1-0	Romania	H
Won	3-0	Armenia	A
Won	2-0	Macedonia	A
Won	4-3	Finland	H
Won	4-0	Andorra	A
Won	8-1	Andorra	H
Won	6-1	Macedonia	H
Lost	2-0	Romania	A
Won	4-1	Armenia	H
Lost	2-0	Holland	H
Won	3-0	Finland	A
Won	1-0	Norway (Play-off)	A
Won	1-0	Norway (Play-off)	H

TOP SCORERS

Jan Koller	9
Tomas Rosicky	7

Jan Koller.

STRONGEST STARTING LINE-UP! 4-4-2

CECH

GRYGERA — ROZEHNAL — UJFALUSI — JANKULOVSKI

POBORSKY — ROSICKY — GALASEK — NEDVED

KOLLER — BAROS

TEAMTALK!

When Czech Republic fell at the semis in Euro 2004, many thought it was the last time this set of players would appear together. But they're back for one more chance and, if Pavel Nedved decides to play on and Jan Koller recovers from a knee injury, all the old guard will be on board. Whatever happens, the Czechs will be brilliant to watch. They were in typical all-out attacking form in qualifying, scoring four or more goals in a game five times, and were only edged out of the top spot by a red-hot Holland.

MATCHMAN'S VERDICT: "WIV A GROUP OF PLAYERS GETTIN' ON A BIT, THIS IS DA CZECH REP'S LAST SHOT AT WC GLORY. IT'S NOW OR NEVER, BOYZ!"

PLAYER TO WATCH!

Milan Baros

Aston Villa star Baros was top scorer at Euro 2004, and he has a big role to play again. The pacy striker started 2006 with a record of 26 goals in 45 Czech Republic games, which shows he's a big danger to defenders!

THE PLAYERS!

GOALKEEPERS

Petr Cech	Chelsea
Jaromir Blazek	Sparta Prague
Antonin Kinsky	Saturn

DEFENDERS

Rene Bolf	Auxerre
Zdenek Grygera	Ajax
Tomas Hubschman	Shakhtar
Marek Jankulovski	AC Milan
Martin Jiranek	Spartak Moscow
Radoslav Kovac	Spartak Moscow
Pavel Mares	Zenit
David Rozehnal	Paris St Germain
Tomas Ujfalusi	Fiorentina

MIDFIELDERS

Tomas Galasek	Ajax
David Jarolim	Hamburg
Jiri Jarosik	Birmingham
Pavel Nedved	Juventus
Jarosil Plasil	Monaco
Karel Poborsky	Ceske Budejovice
Jan Polak	Nuremberg
Tomas Rosicky	Borussia Dortmund
Libor Sionko	Austria Vienna
Tomas Sivok	Sparta Prague
Rudolf Skacel	Hearts
Vladimir Smicer	Bordeaux

STRIKERS

Milan Baros	Aston Villa
Tomas Jun	Trabzonspor
Jan Koller	Borussia Dortmund
Marek Heinz	Galatasaray
Vratislav Lokvenc	Salzburg
Jiri Stajner	Hannover

USA!

| COACH! | BRUCE ARENA | WORLD RANKING! | 7th | WORLD CUP ODDS! | 100/1 | WORLD CUP BEST! | SEMI-FINAL 1930 |

⭐ STRONGEST STARTING LINE-UP! 4-4-2

KELLER

HEJDUK — POPE — BERHALTER — BOCANEGRA

DEMPSEY — DONOVAN — BEASLEY — CONVEY

McBRIDE — JOHNSON

⭐ ROAD TO THE FINALS!

Stage 2 Group 1	P	W	D	L	F	A	Pts
USA	6	3	3	0	13	3	12
Panama	6	2	2	2	8	11	8
Jamaica	6	1	4	1	7	5	7
El Salvador	6	1	1	4	2	11	4

Stage 3	P	W	D	L	F	A	Pts
USA	10	7	1	2	16	6	22
Mexico	10	7	1	2	22	9	22
Costa Rica	10	5	1	4	15	14	16
Trinidad & Tobago	10	4	1	5	10	15	13
Guatemala	10	3	2	5	16	18	11
Panama	10	0	2	8	4	21	2

RESULT	SCORE	OPPOSITION	H/A
Won	3-0	Grenada	H
Won	3-2	Grenada	A
Drew	1-1	Jamaica	A
Won	2-0	El Salvador	H
Drew	1-1	Panama	A
Won	2-0	El Salvador	A
Won	6-0	Panama	H
Drew	1-1	Jamaica	H
Won	2-1	Trinidad & Tobago	A
Lost	2-1	Mexico	A
Won	2-0	Guatemala	H
Won	3-0	Costa Rica	H
Won	3-0	Panama	A
Won	1-0	Trinidad & Tobago	H
Won	2-0	Mexico	H
Drew	0-0	Guatemala	A
Lost	3-0	Costa Rica	A
Won	2-0	Panama	H

TOP SCORERS	
Landon Donovan	7
Ed Johnson	7

⭐ TEAMTALK!

After years of steady improvement the USA should be taken seriously. The team is ranked inside the top ten in world footy, and qualified for Germany with three games to spare! Qualification was secured with a 2-0 home win over arch-rivals Mexico – Steve Ralston and DaMarcus Beasley scoring to wrap up a famous victory and sneak top spot on goal difference. But coach Bruce Arena is realistic – with Italy, Czech Republic and Ghana to face, reaching the knockout stage would be an achievement.

MATCHMAN'S VERDICT: "USA ARE A MAJOR FORCE IN WORLD FOOTY THESE DAYS, BUT DA STARS 'N' STRIPES HAVE A TOUGH JOB JUST TO GET OUT OF DA GROUP!"

⭐ PLAYER TO WATCH!

Landon Donovan

Donovan is only 24 years old, but has over 70 caps already! The high-scoring midfielder, who claimed seven goals in qualifying, will be playing in his second World Cup. He's one reason why the USA are full of confidence right now!

GHANA!

| COACH! | RATOMIR DUJKOVIC | WORLD RANKING! | 50th | WORLD CUP ODDS! | 200/1 | WORLD CUP BEST! | DEBUT IN FINALS |

⭐ STRONGEST STARTING LINE-UP! 4-4-2

ADJEI

PANTSIL — KUFFOUR — MENSAH — PAPPOE

KINGSTON — APPIAH — ESSIEN — MUNTARI

ASAMOAH — AMOAH

⭐ ROAD TO THE FINALS!

Stage 3	P	W	D	L	F	A	Pts
Ghana	10	6	3	1	17	4	21
Congo	10	4	4	2	14	10	16
South Africa	10	5	1	4	12	14	16
Burkina Faso	10	4	1	5	14	13	13
Cape Verde Islands	10	3	1	6	8	15	10
Uganda	10	2	2	6	6	15	8

RESULT	SCORE	OPPOSITION	H/A
Won	5-0	Somalia (play-off)	A
Won	2-0	Somalia (play-off)	H
Lost	1-0	Burkina Faso	A
Won	3-0	South Africa	H
Drew	1-1	Uganda	A
Won	2-0	Cape Verde Islands	H
Drew	0-0	Congo	H
Drew	1-1	Congo	A
Won	2-1	Burkina Faso	H
Won	2-0	South Africa	A
Won	2-0	Uganda	H
Won	4-0	Cape Verde Islands	A

TOP SCORERS	
Gyan Asamoah	4
Stephen Appiah	4

⭐ TEAMTALK!

Ghana have qualified for the World Cup finals for the first time ever – and have been handed a tough draw as a reward! But this team only lost once in 12 matches in qualifying, and that demands respect. Ghana's real strength is midfield, where Chelsea's Michael Essien joins Stephen Appiah and Sulley Ali Muntari. But on the downside, Ghana lack a convincing goalscorer and their form earlier in 2006 wasn't so good – they lost two out of three games in the African Cup Of Nations. Can they improve?

MATCHMAN'S VERDICT: "IT'S A WELL TRICKY DEBUT FOR GHANA, INNIT? THE AFRICANS WILL BE UP FOR CAUSING A SHOCK OR TWO, SO WATCH OUT FOR THEM!"

⭐ PLAYER TO WATCH!

Stephen Appiah

Appiah is Ghana's captain and, with Michael Essien, the focus of the team's midfield. He knows group rivals Italy inside out after spells in Serie A with Udinese, Brescia and Juventus. Appiah is a tough-tackler who scores goals.

Matthew Amoah.

THIS IS THE FIRST HALF OF ME WORLD CUP QUIZ! HOW MUCH DO YA KNOW ABOUT THE MOST BLINGIN' COMP ON THE PLANET?

HEAD SPIN!

WHICH LEGENDARY ENGLAND STRIKER HAS BEEN ALL MESSED UP 'ERE? HAVE A GUESS!

ANSWER

10 POINTS FOR CORRECT ANSWER

MY SCORE /10

LEGENDS MATCH-UP!

CAN YA MATCH UP THESE WICKED WORLD CUP HEROES WIV THE COUNTRY THEY PLAYED FOR?

 1. JOHAN CRUYFF — A. ROMANIA

 2. ROBERTO BAGGIO — B. GERMANY

 3. RUDI VOELLER — C. ARGENTINA

 4. GHEORGHE HAGI — D. ITALY

 5. MARIO KEMPES — E. HOLLAND

2 POINTS FOR EACH CORRECT ANSWER

MY SCORE /10

SPOT THE DIFFERENCE!

CAN YA SPOT DA FIVE DIFFERENCES BETWEEN THESE TWO FLASH PICS?

2 POINTS FOR EACH CORRECT ANSWER

MY SCORE /10

WORLD CUP WINNERS!

FIVE OF THESE TEAMS 'AVE WON DA WORLD CUP, BUT DO YA KNOW WHICH ONES? HAVE A POP AT IT!

 BRAZIL
 ARGENTINA
 HOLLAND
 ENGLAND
 ITALY
 SPAIN
 URUGUAY
 MEXICO

2 POINTS FOR EACH CORRECT ANSWER

MY SCORE /10

CROSSWORD!

FILL IN DA BOXES, THEN SORT DA LETTERS IN THE GOLD SQUARES TO SPELL THE SURNAME OF A 1966 HERO!

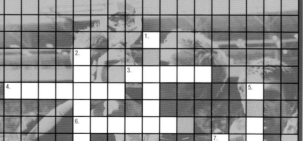

ACROSS

3. England legend Paul Gascoigne's famous nickname!
4. First winners of the World Cup!
6. Brazil and Real Madrid number 9!
8. Baldy France star – ZZ!
9. The 2006 World Cup hosts!
10. Surname of the highest-ever scorer in World Cup history!

DOWN

1. Current world champions!
2. Former England left-back, now Man. City's manager!
5. Wolves boss who played for and managed England!
7. World Cup hosts in 1990!

Write the 'Goalden Word' below and bag five extra points!

GOALDEN WORD

½ POINT FOR EACH CORRECT ANSWER + 5 FOR GOALDEN WORD

MY SCORE /10

QUIZ!

FINAL APPEARANCES!

 1 BRAZIL **2 ENGLAND** **3 LATVIA** **4 ITALY** **5 WALES**

MATCH THESE TEAMS UP WITH HOW MANY TIMES THEY'VE PLAYED IN THE WORLD CUP FINALS!

2 POINTS FOR EACH CORRECT ANSWER

a 1   **b** 11   **c** 15   **d** 0   **e** 17

MY SCORE /10

DR. FOOTY'S FACTS!

READ MY ENGLAND FACTS BELOW AND CROSS THE FALSE ONE!

1. Michael Owen's first World Cup goal was against Argentina!

2. Geoff Hurst scored a hat-trick in the 1966 World Cup final!

3. England failed to qualify for the 1994 World Cup finals in the USA!

10 POINTS FOR CORRECT ANSWER   MY SCORE /10

MARADONA QUIZ!

FOOTY LEGEND MARADONA IS ONE OF DA WICKEDEST PLAYERS EVER, BUT HOW MUCH DO YA KNOW ABOUT HIM?

1 Which ace country did he play for?
ANSWER

2 What year did he score his famous 'Hand Of God' goal against England?
ANSWER

3 He was a hero at which Italian club – Roma or Napoli?
ANSWER

4 What is Maradona's first name?
ANSWER

5 True or False? Maradona played for Spanish giants Real Madrid.
ANSWER

2 POINTS FOR EACH CORRECT ANSWER   MY SCORE /10

WORDSEARCH!

CHECK THIS OUT! THERE ARE 20 FOOTY LEGENDS OR WORLD CUP WORDS HIDDEN BELOW! GO FIND 'EM!

```
U Q G D V J V D G I P G B J U U Y B W C
T T M A D C V W M Z Y I P N N T E L F B
J O B A Z L L F T U C E X Q R E N G L E
L O E P N Z R X Z Z L F R R E M I N V C
X B C X A Z N Z E X L A U K I A X O K
K N K R B Q C F E Q N T Y M I R T K K H
U E E L O I B K R E H H F H R S N X H A
V D N M Y N Q R A B Y H B E T E O U C M
T L B T J G A A R Y P A P X S L F Q I Q
O O A M D F Y L W I N C S I M U E L O R
M G U I P A L A D K B H E D Q J W H T E
Q W E C E P D D S O A O T I L U N N S E
S B R I Q D L X I Z L O A Z P Q E O G V
G U H C L B R A Z I L R R N L K A T C H
S I A E S S O W T R O B C W X C Z L A O
T L W H U O L R F I R F O P M Y J R R X
C C S K T O R I S K N S S A K P Y A E Q
Y I E G Q T F I Z H A I G I Y Q E H C D
W R X V O W A R J B B B K C M L W W C A Y
O O T S M F D M E T S R Z M Z T N K N I
```

>> BANKS
>> BECKENBAUER
>> BECKHAM
>> BRAZIL
>> CARECA
>> CHARLTON
>> FONTAINE
>> GAZZA
>> GOLDEN BOOT
>> JULES RIMET
>> MATTHAUS
>> PELE
>> PIQUE
>> PLATINI
>> RONALDO
>> SOCRATES
>> STOICHKOV
>> STRIKER
>> SUKER
>> WADDLE

½ POINT FOR EACH CORRECT ANSWER   MY SCORE /10

ITALY OR SPAIN?

 1. PAOLO ROSSI
ANSWER

 2. EMILIO BUTRAGUENO
ANSWER

 3. ANDONI ZUBIZARRETA
ANSWER

 **4. FRANCO BARESI**
ANSWER

 5. DINO ZOFF
ANSWER

THESE TWO TEAMS 'AVE HAD SOME WELL GOOD PLAYERS OVER DA YEARS! BUT WHO PLAYED FOR WHO? WRITE YER ANSWERS IN DA BOXES!

2 POINTS FOR EACH CORRECT ANSWER   MY SCORE /10

ANSWERS!

BRAZIL!

| COACH! | CARLOS ALBERTO PERREIRA | CAPTAIN! | CAFU | MOST CAPS! | CAFU 144 |

⭐ QUALIFYING FORM! ⭐

Even for Brazil, qualifying wasn't easy – the team drew seven and lost two of their 18 games, which includes a shocking 1-0 defeat to Ecuador and a 3-1 loss against Argentina. Coach Carlos Alberto Perreira switched the team around loads, which didn't help!

⭐ STRENGTHS! ⭐

Brazil have world-class players in almost every position – and a few more in reserve, too! Their attacking threat is huge, and if everyone is on form they'll be almost unstoppable. It's going to take a top, top team to knock Brazil out of the tournament!

⭐ WEAKNESSES! ⭐

Brazil aren't invincible. Their 'keepers are prone to bad mistakes, and the defence can be a bit dodgy as well. Full-backs Cafu and Roberto Carlos are getting on a bit and Roque Junior has the odd nightmare in the centre of defence. If the midfield attacks too much, it leaves big gaps in the team.

Robinho.

⭐ CAN THEY WIN? ⭐

Too right they can, and Brazil are massive faves to keep their trophy and make it six World Cup wins! The class of their starting line-up, along with the talent crammed on to the bench, means any team beating Brazil will have to play out of this world or catch them on an off day. And it isn't very often that Ronaldo and his mates all play badly at once!

MATCHMAN'S VERDICT: "DA SAMBA STARS ARE LOOKIN' HOT AN' BRAZIL CAN WHUP ANYONE! SO, WHO'S GONNA STOP 'EM? IT'S SCARY!"

⭐ RESULTS AND LINE-UPS IN QUALIFYING!

COLOMBIA	ECUADOR	PERU	URUGUAY	PARAGUAY	ARGENTINA	CHILE	BOLIVIA	VENEZUELA
Won 2-1 (a)	*Won 1-0 (h)*	*Drew 1-1 (a)*	*Drew 3-3 (h)*	*Drew 0-0 (a)*	*Won 3-1 (h)*	*Drew 1-1 (a)*	*Won 3-1 (h)*	*Won 5-2 (a)*
Dida	Dida	Dida	Dida	Dida	Dida	Dida	Julio Cesar	Dida
Cafu	Cafu	Cafu	Cafu	Cafu	Cafu	Cafu	Belletti	Cafu
Lucio	Lucio	Lucio	Lucio	Lucio	Juan	Juan	Edmilson	Juan
Roque Junior	Roque Junior	Roque Junior	Roque Junior	Roque Junior	Roque Junior	Roque Junior	Roque Junior	Roque Junior
Roberto Carlos	Roberto Carlos	Junior	Junior	Roberto Carlos	Roberto Carlos	Roberto Carlos	Roberto Carlos	Roberto Carlos
Gilberto	Gilberto	Gilberto	Renato	Renato	Edmilson	Edmilson	Juninho	Renato
Emerson	Ronaldinho 1	Kaka	Kaka 1	Ronaldinho	Juninho	Juninho	Edu	Kaka 2
Alex	Emerson	Emerson	Gilberto	Gilberto	Kaka	Kaka	Gilberto	Juninho
Ze Roberto	Ze Roberto	Ze Roberto	Ze Roberto	Ze Roberto	Ze Roberto	Edu	Ronaldinho 1	Ronaldo 2
Rivaldo	Rivaldo	Rivaldo 1	Rivaldo	Kaka	Luis Fabiano	Luis Fabiano 1	Ronaldo 1	Ronaldinho
Ronaldo 1	Ronaldo	Ronaldo	Ronaldo 2	Ronaldo	Ronaldo 3	Ronaldo	Adriano 1	Ze Roberto
Substitutes:	**Substitutes:**	**Substitutes:**	**Substitutes:**	**Substitutes:**	**Substitutes:**	**Substitutes:**	**Substitutes:**	**Substitutes:**
Renato 60	Renato 62	Emerson 61	Alex 72	Juninho 67	Alex 74	Julio Baptista 72	Alex 60	Edu
Kaka 1 60	Kaka 68	Kaka 74	Juninho 79		Julio Baptista 74	Gilberto 80	Renato 60	Adriano 1
Diego 60	Alex 90	Rivaldo 81	Luis Fabiano 79		Edu 90	Alex 85	Robinho 73	Alex

WORLD CUP FINALS 2006 — GROUP F

MOST GOALS!	RONALDO 60	WORLD RANKING!	1ST	WORLD CUP ODDS!	11/4	WORLD CUP BEST!	WINNERS 1958, 1962, 1970, 1994, 2002

⭐ PLAYER TO WATCH! ⭐

Adriano
If defenders stop Ronaldo, they've still got Adriano to deal with! The big striker has an awesome left foot and can score goals from way out. A hat-trick against Chile in qualifying showed his ability.

⭐ STRONGEST STARTING LINE-UP! 4-4-2 ⭐

DIDA

CAFU — ROQUE JUNIOR — LUCIO — CARLOS

ROBINHO — EMERSON — KAKA — ZE ROBERTO

RONALDO — RONALDINHO

⭐ PLAYER TO WATCH! ⭐

Ronaldinho
Ronaldinho went to the 2002 World Cup in the shadow of Ronaldo, but then his goal knocked England out in the quarter-finals, and the rest is history. The Barcelona star is the best player in the world – fact!

⭐ ROAD TO THE FINALS!

South America	P	W	D	L	F	A	Pts
Brazil	18	9	7	2	35	17	34
Argentina	18	10	4	4	29	17	34
Ecuador	18	8	4	6	23	19	28
Paraguay	18	8	4	6	23	23	28
Uruguay	18	6	7	5	23	28	25
Colombia	18	6	6	6	24	16	24
Chile	18	5	7	6	18	22	22
Venezuela	18	5	3	10	20	28	18
Peru	18	4	6	8	20	28	18
Bolivia	18	4	2	12	20	37	14

TOP SCORERS	
Ronaldo	10
Adriano	6

Ronaldo.

⭐ THE PLAYERS!

GOALKEEPERS	
Julio Cesar	Inter Milan
Dida	AC Milan
Marcos	Palmeiras

DEFENDERS	
Juliano Belletti	Barcelona
Cafu	AC Milan
Roberto Carlos	Real Madrid
Cicinho	Real Madrid
Gilberto da Silva	Hertha Berlin
Gustavo Nery	Corinthians
Juan	Bayer Leverkusen
Lucio	Bayern Munich
Luisao	Benfica
Roque Junior	Bayer Leverkusen

MIDFIELDERS	
Alex	Fenerbahce
Julio Baptista	Real Madrid
Edmilson	Barcelona
Edu	Valencia
Emerson	Juventus
Gilberto	Arsenal
Juninho	Lyon
Kaka	AC Milan
Renato	Sevilla
Ricardinho	Corinthians
Ze Roberto	Bayern Munich

STRIKERS	
Adriano	Inter Milan
Luis Fabiano	Sevilla
Ricardo Oliveira	Real Betis
Robinho	Real Madrid
Ronaldinho	Barcelona
Ronaldo	Real Madrid

RESULTS AND LINE-UPS IN QUALIFYING!

COLOMBIA	ECUADOR	PERU	URUGUAY	PARAGUAY	ARGENTINA	CHILE	BOLIVIA	VENEZUELA
Drew 0-0 (h)	Lost 1-0 (a)	Won 1-0 (h)	Drew 1-1 (h)	Won 4-1 (h)	Lost 3-1 (a)	Won 5-0 (h)	Drew 1-1 (a)	Won 3-0 (h)
...da	Dida	Dida	Dida	Dida	Dida	Dida	Julio Cesar	Dida
...fu	Cafu	Cafu	Cafu	Belletti	Cafu	Cafu	Cicinho	Cafu
...an	Juan	Lucio	Lucio	Lucio	Juan	Lucio	Luisao	Lucio
...que Junior	Roque Junior	Juan	Luisao	Roque Junior	Roque Junior	Juan 1	Roque Junior	Juan
...berto Carlos	Roberto Carlos	Roberto Carlos	Roberto Carlos	Roberto Carlos	Roberto Carlos 1	Roberto Carlos	Gilberto S	Roberto Carlos 1
...nato	Renato	Emerson	Emerson 1	Emerson	Emerson	Emerson	Gilberto	Emerson
...ex	Juninho	Juninho	Ronaldinho	Robinho 1	Robinho	Robinho 1	Ricardinho	Ronaldinho
...agrao	Kaka	Kaka 1	Kaka	Kaka	Kaka	Kaka	Juninho 1	Kaka
...Roberto	Kleberson	Ze Roberto	Ze Roberto	Ze Roberto 1	Ze Roberto	Ze Roberto	Renato	Ze Roberto
...naldinho	Ronaldinho	Ronaldinho	Ricardo Oliveira	Ronaldinho 2	Ronaldinho	Adriano 3	Robinho	Adriano 1
...naldo	Ronaldo	Ronaldo	Ronaldo	Adriano	Adriano	Ronaldo	Adriano	Ronaldo 1

Substitutes:		Substitutes:		Substitutes:		Substitutes:		Substitutes:		Substitutes:		Substitutes:		Substitutes:		Substitutes:	
...ano	58	Ricardinho	64	Robinho	46	Robinho	63	Gilberto	75	Renato	61	Ricardinho	45	Gustavo Nery	58	Robinho	64
...driano	58	Dudu	74	Renato	83	Renato	68	Ricardo Oliveira	75			Gilberto	59	Alex	58	Alex	64
	84	Adriano	81					Juan	82			Juninho	66	Julio Baptista	79	Juninho	68

Kaka.

AUSTRALIA!

COACH!	GUUS HIDDINK	WORLD RANKING!	49TH	WORLD CUP ODDS!	125/1	WORLD CUP BEST!	FIRST ROUND 1974

Tim Cahill (second left).

ROAD TO THE FINALS!

Oceania	P	W	D	L	F	A	Pts
Australia	5	4	1	0	21	3	13
Sol. Islands	5	3	1	1	9	6	10
New Zealand	5	3	0	2	17	5	9
Fiji	5	1	1	3	3	10	4
Tahiti	5	1	1	3	2	24	4
Vanuatu	5	1	0	4	5	9	3

RESULT	SCORE	OPPOSITION	H/A
Won	1-0	New Zealand	H
Won	9-0	Tahiti	H
Won	6-1	Fiji	H
Won	3-0	Vanuatu	A
Drew	2-2	Sol. Islands	A
Won	7-0	Sol. Islands (play-off)	H
Won	2-1	Sol. Islands (play-off)	A
Lost	1-0	Uruguay (play-off)	A
Won	1-0	Uruguay (play-off)	H
		won 4-2 on pens	

TOP SCORERS

Tim Cahill	7
Brett Emerton	4
Mile Sterjovski	3

Mark Viduka.

THE PLAYERS!

GOALKEEPERS

Brad Jones	Middlesbrough
Zeljko Kalac	AC Milan
Mark Schwarzer	Middlesbrough

DEFENDERS

Steve Laybutt	Gent
Jon McKain	Poli Timisoara
Ljubo Milicevic	Thun
Craig Moore	Newcastle
Lucas Neill	Blackburn
Tony Popovic	Crystal Palace
Michael Thwaite	National Bucharest
Luke Wilkshire	Bristol City

MIDFIELDERS

Marco Bresciano	Parma
Alex Brosque	Queensland Roar
Tim Cahill	Everton
Scott Chipperfield	Basel
Jason Culina	Twente
Ahmad Elrich	Fulham
Brett Emerton	Blackburn
Vince Grella	Parma
Harry Kewell	Liverpool
Stan Lazaridis	Birmingham
Josip Skoko	Wigan
Mile Sterjovski	Basel

STRIKERS

Paul Agostino	1860 Munich
John Aloisi	Alaves
Joel Griffiths	Neuchatel Xamax
Ante Milicic	Newcastle United Jets
Archie Thompson	Melbourne Victory
Mark Viduka	Middlesbrough

STRONGEST STARTING LINE-UP! 4-4-2

SCHWARZER

NEILL — VIDMAR — MOORE — MUSCAT

EMERTON — CAHILL — CHIPPERFIELD — KEWELL

VIDUKA — ALOISI

TEAMTALK!

The whole of Australia went footy mad after they defeated Uruguay in a play-off to reach their first World Cup finals since 1974! But although they're chuffed just to be there, they won't go to Germany to make up the numbers. Experienced coach Guus Hiddink is a miracle worker after taking South Korea to the semis in 2002, and with plenty of pace and ability going forward, he'll be looking for his side to spring a few surprises this summer. On their day, Australia are a match for any team!

MATCHMAN'S VERDICT:
"AUSSIES RULE! WELL, MAYBE NOT AT DIS WORLD CUP, BUT THEY'LL GIVE IT A GOOD GO AND COULD CAUSE A SHOCK!"

PLAYER TO WATCH!

Harry Kewell

The flying Liverpool winger is back in top form – and that's great news for Australia. At his best, Kewell can be world class and cause real problems with his trickery from the left wing and wicked balls into the strikers!

CROATIA!

| COACH! | ZLATKO KRANJCAR | WORLD RANKING! | 20TH | WORLD CUP ODDS! | 50/1 | WORLD CUP BEST! | SEMI-FINALS 1998 |

★ STRONGEST STARTING LINE-UP! 4-4-2

BUTINA

SIMIC — TUDOR — SIMUNIC — R. KOVAC

SRNA — N. KOVAC — BABIC — KRANJCAR

KLASNIC — PRSO

★ ROAD TO THE FINALS! ★

Group 8 Europe	P	W	D	L	F	A	Pts
Croatia	10	7	3	0	21	5	24
Sweden	10	8	0	2	30	4	24
Bulgaria	10	4	3	3	17	17	15
Hungary	10	4	2	4	13	14	14
Iceland	10	1	1	8	14	27	4
Malta	10	0	3	7	4	32	3

RESULT	SCORE	OPPOSITION	H/A
Won	3-0	Hungary	H
Won	0-1	Sweden	A
Drew	2-2	Bulgaria	H
Won	4-0	Icelend	H
Won	3-0	Malta	H
Won	1-3	Bulgaria	A
Won	1-3	Iceland	A
Drew	1-1	Malta	A
Won	1-0	Sweden	H
Drew	0-0	Hungary	A

TOP SCORERS	
Dario Srna	5
Dado Prso	5

Dario Srna.

★ TEAMTALK! ★

Croatia look a much better side going into this summer's World Cup than the poor excuse for a footy team that England battered 4-2 at Euro 2004. Zlatko Kranjcar's side went through their qualifying campaign unbeaten, winning seven and drawing three games, and beating second-placed Sweden twice. They're tough at the back, and with tricky wide midfielder Dario Srna providing the bullets for wicked Rangers striker Dado Prso, Croatia will be confident of making progress in the finals!

MATCHMAN'S VERDICT: "DA COOL CROATIANS WERE WICKED IN QUALIFYING, 'AN IF THEY CAN KEEP UP THAT FORM THEY'LL BE WELL 'ARD TO BEAT IN GERMANY!"

★ PLAYER TO WATCH! ★

Dado Prso
Prso is the best-known Croatian player in the squad, and the strong targetman will lead the attack in the World Cup. He's awesome in the air but can also keep possession, holding it up to bring attacking team-mates into play!

JAPAN!

| COACH! | ZICO | WORLD RANKING! | 15TH | WORLD CUP ODDS! | 150/1 | WORLD CUP BEST! | SECOND ROUND 2002 |

★ STRONGEST STARTING LINE-UP! 4-4-2

KAWAGUCHI

KAJI — MIYAMOTO — NAKAZAWA — ALEX

NAKAMURA — NAKATA — ONO — FUKUNISHI

YANAGISAWA — TAMADA

★ ROAD TO THE FINALS! ★

Asia Group 2	P	W	D	L	F	A	Pts
Japan	6	5	0	1	9	4	15
Iran	6	4	1	1	7	3	13
Bahrain	6	1	1	4	4	7	4
North Korea	6	1	0	5	5	11	3

RESULT	SCORE	OPPOSITION	H/A
Won	2-1	North Korea	H
Lost	2-1	Iran	A
Won	1-0	Bahrain	H
Won	1-0	Bahrain	A
Won	2-0	North Korea	A
Won	2-1	Iran	H

TOP SCORERS	
Takashi Fukunishi	3
Mitsuo Ogasawara	3
Masashi Oguro	3
Takayaki Suzuki	3

Hidetoshi Nakata.

★ TEAMTALK! ★

After doing so well to reach the second round of World Cup 2002, Japan struggled to even qualify for World Cup 2006. Brazil legend Zico took over as coach but even he found it hard to get results, and the team very nearly crashed out in the first qualifying group stage – they only made it thanks to late wins against Oman and North Korea. They topped the second qualifying group, which also featured Iran, but they'll find the going much tougher alongside Brazil, Croatia and Australia!

MATCHMAN'S VERDICT: "I IS A BIG FAN OF JAPAN, WIV NAKATA AN' DA BOYZ SHOWING THEIR SKILLS! BUT THEY'LL STRUGGLE AND COULD BE ON AN EARLY PLANE!"

★ PLAYER TO WATCH! ★

Shinji Ono
The Red Diamonds ace has overtaken Hidetoshi Nakata as Japan's star man. The attacking midfielder has a great touch, brilliant vision and loves to put killer balls through for his strikers! He likes to get forward and score, too.

MATCHMAN'S

IT'S PART TWO OF ME TRICKY WORLD CUP TEST! THIS IS WHERE WE SEE WOT YA KNOW ABOUT DA BLINGIN' WORLD STARS!

NATIONAL DRESS!

WHICH MEGA-TALENTED STRIKER 'AS DRESSED HIMSELF UP AS A SCARY VIKING WARRIOR?

ANSWER

10 POINTS FOR CORRECT ANSWER

MY SCORE /10

MICHAEL BALLACK QUIZ!

WOT DO YA KNOW 'BOUT GERMANY'S STAR PLAYER? HAVE A CRACK AT THESE FIVE QUESTIONS FOR TEN POINTS!

1 At which club did he play before Bayern snapped him up?

ANSWER

2 How much did Bayern pay to sign him – was it £4.2 million or £14.2 million?

ANSWER

3 When did he make his Germany debut – 1999, 2001 or 2003?

ANSWER

4 What's his favourite position – right-wing or centre midfield?

ANSWER

5 True or False? He's Germany's captain.

ANSWER

2 POINTS FOR EACH CORRECT ANSWER

MY SCORE /10

CHANGIN' SHIRTS!

TWO OF THESE TOP TRICKSTERS HAVE CHANGED SHIRTS – LINK 'EM UP WITH AN ARROW!

DECO

HATEM TRABELSI

ASHLEY COLE

JUAN PABLO SORIN

ZINEDINE ZIDANE

ALBERTO GILARDINO

5 POINTS FOR EACH CORRECT ANSWER

MY SCORE /10

DEBUT BOYS!

CAN YA MATCH THESE WORLD CUP FIRST TIMERS WIV DA COUNTRY THEY WILL BE PLAYIN' FOR?

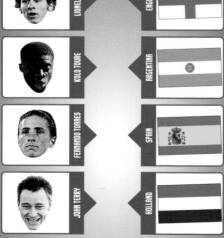

LIONEL MESSI — ENGLAND

KOLO TOURE — ARGENTINA

FERNANDO TORRES — SPAIN

JOHN TERRY — HOLLAND

WESLEY SNEIJDER — IVORY COAST

2 POINTS FOR EACH CORRECT ANSWER

MY SCORE /10

CROSSWORD!

FIGURE OUT DA CROSSWORD, THEN REARRANGE DA GOLD SQUARES TO REVEAL A WORLD SUPERSTAR!

ACROSS

3. Awesome Brazil star Adriano plays in this position!

5. Age of Spain's Fernando Torres!

7. Forward who plays for Argentina and Corinthians!

8. Portugal and Inter Milan winger!

9. Holland's _____ van der Vaart!

10. Italy defender Fabio Cannavaro plays for this top club team!

DOWN

1. Portugal's Maniche left this club to join Chelsea in 2006!

2. Spain striker Fernando Morientes is ? years old!

4. England striker's third WC!

6. Dirk Kuyt's national team!

Bag five points by using the gold letters to spell a top defender!

GOALDEN WORD

½ POINT FOR EACH CORRECT ANSWER + 5 FOR GOALDEN WORD

MY SCORE /10

QUIZ!

NOW GO TO PAGE 62 FOR EXTRA TIME IN QUIZLAND!

1ST HALF SCORE!	2ND HALF SCORE!
/100	/100

SPOT THE DIFFERENCE!

SCAN YER EYES OVER THESE PICS AND CIRCLE DA FIVE DIFFERENCES!

2 POINTS FOR EACH CORRECT ANSWER — MY SCORE /10

HELP PERCY!

HELLO! CAN YOU HELP ME PUT THESE TWICKY NAMES BACK AS THEY SHOULD BE?

1. Jean-loogey Buffoon — ANSWER
2. See-base-tin Diesel-her — ANSWER
3. Part-thick V-hairer — ANSWER
4. Hand-rayers I-sack-some — ANSWER
5. Crisp-piano Ronald-doh — ANSWER

2 POINTS FOR EACH CORRECT ANSWER — MY SCORE /10

BEHIND THE LEGEND!

CAN YA TELL WHICH OF ME TOP FOOTY MATES IS HIDIN' BEHIND DA FACE OF ENGLAND LEGEND BOBBY CHARLTON?

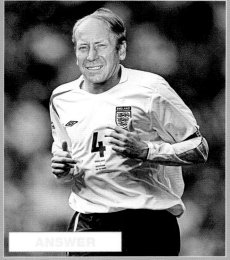

ANSWER

> 1. I'm a versatile midfielder!
> 2. I scored loads for my club this season!
> 3. I was injured for the last World Cup!

10 POINTS FOR CORRECT ANSWER — MY SCORE /10

dream team!

CAN YA WORK OUT DA PLAYERS I'VE PICKED TO KICK IT IN ME WORLD CUP XI? USE DA CLUES AN' THINK HARD!

The Blues' 'Czech' mate!
GK — ANSWER

Brazil's 35-year-old legend!
RB — ANSWER

Barcelona & Spain mop-top!
CB — ANSWER

England & Man. United ace!
CB — Rio Ferdinand

Versatile Italy full-back – GZ!
LB — ANSWER

AC Milan & Brazil playmaker!
RM — ANSWER

France tough guy – CM!
CM — ANSWER

Chelsea & England penalty king!
CM — ANSWER

Arsenal & Spain trickster!
LM — ANSWER

Ukraine goal king – AS!
S — ANSWER

Trinidad & Tobago hero – DY!
S — ANSWER

1 POINT FOR EACH CORRECT ANSWER — MY SCORE /10

DEFENDER OR PRETENDER?

1. MICHEL SALGADO — ANSWER
2. LUCA TONI — ANSWER
3. JUAN RIQUELME — ANSWER
4. JORGE ANDRADE — ANSWER
5. SOL CAMPBELL — ANSWER

CHECK THIS STACK OF FOOTY STARS, AND WRITE DEFENDER BY THE DUDES WOT PLAY AT DA BACK AND PRETENDER BY THOSE WHO DON'T!

2 POINTS FOR EACH CORRECT ANSWER — MY SCORE /10

ANSWERS!

SPOT THE DIFFERENCE! 1. Stripes on Crespo's shorts missing; 2. Crespo's right foot missing; 3. Ball is green; 4. Cafu's captain armband missing; 5. Cafu's left sock is all blue.

GOLDEN WORD: William Gallas.

DEFENDER OR PRETENDER? Defender – Michel Salgado, Jorge Andrade, Sol Campbell. Pretender – Luca Toni, Juan Riquelme.

BEHIND THE LEGEND! Steven Gerrard.

DREAM TEAM: GK: Petr Cech; RB: Cafu; CB: Carlos Puyol; LB: Gianluca Zambrotta; RM: Kaka; CM: Claude Makelele; CM: Frank Lampard; LM: Jose Reyes; S: Andriy Shevchenko; S: Dwight Yorke.

CROSSWORD! ACROSS: 3. Striker; 5. Twenty two; 7. Carlos Tevez; 8. Luis Figo; 9. Rafael; 10. Juventus. DOWN: 1. Dinamo Moscow; 2. Thirty; 4. Michael Owen; 6. Holland.

MICHAEL BALLACK QUIZ! 1. Bayer Leverkusen; 2. £4.2 million; 3. 1999; 4. Centre midfield; 5. True.

CHANGIN' SHIRTS! Juan Pablo Sorin & Alberto Gilardino.

DEBUT BOYS! Lionel Messi – Argentina; Kolo Toure – Ivory Coast; Fernando Torres – Spain; John Terry – England; Wesley Sneijder – Holland.

HELP PERCY! 1. Gianluigi Buffon; 2. Sebastian Deisler; 3. Patrick Vieira; 4. Andreas Isaksson; 5. Cristiano Ronaldo.

NATIONAL DRESS! Zlatan Ibrahimovic (Sweden).

FRANCE!

COACH!	RAYMOND DOMENECH	CAPTAIN!	ZINEDINE ZIDANE	MOST CAPS!	LILIAN THURAM 110

⭐ QUALIFYING FORM! ⭐

For a team who are so good on paper, France weren't quite so hot in their campaign! Yes, they topped their group, finishing unbeaten, but they drew both games with Israel and Switzerland and couldn't beat the Republic Of Ireland at home.

⭐ STRENGTHS! ⭐

With Thierry Henry, David Trezeguet, Zinedine Zidane, Djibril Cisse and more, France will be a threat going forward. Getting stars like Zidane, Lilian Thuram and Claude Makelele to come out of retirement was a big plus for the 1998 champions!

⭐ WEAKNESSES! ⭐

France are going through changes as the oldies are replaced by younger players. But Raymond Domenech had to persuade three stars to come out of retirement, which shows a lack of overall quality in the squad. If those veterans pick up injuries during the tournament, France may struggle!

Lilian Thuram.

⭐ CAN THEY WIN? ⭐

Man for man, there aren't many better teams than France! But they need everyone to be on top form. Too many of their stars weren't at their best for the 2002 World Cup and Euro 2004, and it showed in their disappointing results. But if the French play to their potential, they're one of four or five teams who could go on and win the trophy!

MATCHMAN'S VERDICT: "DA FRENCH FRIES 'AVE ALL DA TALENT, BUT DON'T ALWAYS PRODUCE DA GOODS. I RECKS IT'S SEMIS AT BEST 'ERE!"

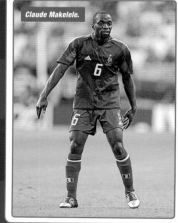
Claude Makelele.

⭐ RESULTS AND LINE-UPS IN QUALIFYING!

ISRAEL	FAROE ISLANDS	REP. OF IRELAND	CYPRUS	SWITZERLAND	ISRAEL
Drew 0-0 (h)	*Won 2-0 (a)*	*Drew 0-0 (h)*	*Won 2-0 (a)*	*Drew 0-0 (h)*	*Drew 1-1 (a)*
Coupet	Coupet	Barthez	Barthez	Barthez	Barthez
Givet	Givet	Givet	Givet	Sagnol	Sagnol
Evra	Evra	Silvestre	Silvestre	Givet	Givet
Gallas	Gallas	Gallas	Gallas	Gallas	Gallas
Squilaci	Squilaci	Squilaci	Squilaci	Boumsong	Boumsong
Mendy	Giuly 1	Wiltord	Wiltord 1	Giuly	Malouda
Makelele	Vieira	Dacourt	Dacourt	Pedretti	Diarra
Vieira	Pedretti	Mavuba	Vieira	Vieira	Vieira
Rothen	Pires	Pires	Pires	Dhorasoo	Pedretti
Henry	Henry	Henry	Henry 1	Wiltord	Wiltord
Saha	Saha	Cisse	Luyindula	Trezeguet	Trezeguet 1
Substitutes:	**Substitutes:**	**Substitutes:**	**Substitutes:**	**Substitutes:**	**Substitutes:**
Giuly 58	Cisse 1 8	Diarra 62	Moreira 46	Meriem 58	Dhorasoo
Pires 66	Dhorasoo 63	Govou 81	Evra 66	Govou 81	
		Diarra 90			

MOST GOALS!	HENRY & TREZEGUET 31	WORLD RANKING!	5TH	WORLD CUP ODDS!	10/1	WORLD CUP BEST!	WINNERS 1998

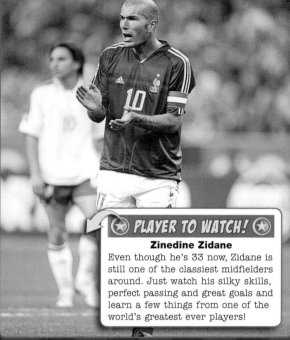

ROAD TO THE FINALS!

Group 4 Europe	P	W	D	L	F	A	Pts
France	10	5	5	0	14	2	20
Switzerland	10	4	6	0	18	7	18
Israel	10	4	6	0	15	10	18
Rep. Of Ireland	10	4	5	1	12	5	17
Cyprus	10	1	1	8	8	20	4
Faroe Islands	10	0	1	9	4	27	1

TOP SCORERS

Djibril Cisse	4
Thierry Henry	2
Sylvain Wiltord	2
Ludovic Giuly	2

Cisse & Wiltord.

PLAYER TO WATCH!

Zinedine Zidane
Even though he's 33 now, Zidane is still one of the classiest midfielders around. Just watch his silky skills, perfect passing and great goals and learn a few things from one of the world's greatest ever players!

STRONGEST STARTING LINE-UP! 4-4-2

BARTHEZ

SAGNOL · THURAM · BOUMSONG · GALLAS

GIULY · MAKELELE · VIEIRA · ZIDANE

HENRY · CISSE

THE PLAYERS!

GOALKEEPERS

Fabien Barthez	Marseille
Gregory Coupet	Lyon
Mickael Landreau	Nantes

DEFENDERS

Eric Abidal	Lyon
Jean Alain Boumsong	Newcastle
Patrice Evra	Man. United
William Gallas	Chelsea
Gael Givet	Monaco
Franck Jurietti	Bordeaux
Anthony Reveillere	Lyon
Willy Sagnol	Bayern Munich
Mikael Silvestre	Man. United
Sebastien Squilaci	Monaco
Lilian Thuram	Juventus

MIDFIELDERS

Vikash Dhorasoo	PSG
Alou Diarra	Lens
Ludovic Giuly	Barcelona
Claude Makelele	Chelsea
Florent Malouda	Lyon
Rio Mavuba	Bordeaux
Camel Meriem	Monaco
Robert Pires	Arsenal
Patrick Vieira	Juventus
Zinedine Zidane	Real Madrid

STRIKERS

Djibril Cisse	Liverpool
Sidney Govou	Lyon
Thierry Henry	Arsenal
Louis Saha	Man. United
David Trezeguet	Juventus
Sylvain Wiltord	Lyon

PLAYER TO WATCH!

Thierry Henry
Henry is one of the best players in the world, but he's never turned on the style at the major tournaments. His pace and ice-cool finishing are made for the world stage, so let's hope he hits top form in Germany!

Patrick Vieira.

	ROE ISLANDS	REP. OF IRELAND	SWITZERLAND	CYPRUS
	Won 3-0* (h)	Won 1-0 (a)	Drew 1-1 (a)	Won 4-0 (h)
pet	Coupet	Coupet	Coupet	Coupet
nol	Sagnol	Sagnol	Reveillere	Sagnol
as	Gallas	Gallas	Gallas	Gallas
ram	Thuram	Thuram	Thuram	Thuram
msong	Boumsong	Boumsong	Boumsong	Boumsong
ouda	Dhorasoo	Dhorasoo	Dhorasoo	Wiltord 1
kelele	Makelele	Makelele	Makelele	Dhorasoo 1
ra	Vieira	Vieira	Vieira	Vieira
ane	Zidane	Zidane	Zidane	Zidane 1
ry	Wiltord	Wiltord	Wiltord	Cisse
se 2	Henry 1	Henry 1	Malouda	Govou

Substitutes:		Substitutes:		Substitutes:		Substitutes:	
orasoo	59	Malouda	70	Cisse 1	46	Diarra	25
tord	67	Cisse	76	Govou	90	Giuly 1	60
ilaci	76	Givet	90			Jurietti	

David Trezeguet.

SWITZERLAND!

| COACH! | KOBI KUHN | WORLD RANKING! | 36TH | WORLD CUP ODDS! | 80/1 | WORLD CUP BEST! | QUARTER-FINALS 1934, 1938, 1954 |

Cabanas, Frei & Barnetta.

ROAD TO THE FINALS!

Group 4 Europe	P	W	D	L	F	A	Pts
France	10	5	5	0	14	2	20
Switzerland	10	4	6	0	18	7	18
Israel	10	4	6	0	15	10	18
Rep. Of Ireland	10	4	5	1	12	5	17
Cyprus	10	1	1	8	8	20	4
Faroe Islands	10	0	1	9	4	27	1

RESULT	SCORE	OPPOSITION	H/A
Won	6-0	Faroe Islands	H
Drew	1-1	Republic Of Ireland	H
Drew	2-2	Israel	A
Drew	0-0	France	A
Won	1-0	Cyprus	H
Won	3-1	Faroe Islands	A
Drew	1-1	Israel	H
Won	3-1	Cyprus	A
Drew	1-1	France	H
Drew	0-0	Republic Of Ireland	A
Won	2-0	Turkey (play-off)	H
Lost	2-4	Turkey (play-off)	A

TOP SCORERS

Alexander Frei	7
Johan Vonlanthen	4

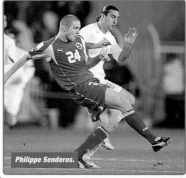

Philippe Senderos.

STRONGEST STARTING LINE-UP! 4-4-2

ZUBERBUEHLER

MAGNIN — DEGEN — SENDEROS — MUELLER

BARNETTA — CABANAS — VOGEL — GYGAX

VONLANTHEN — FREI

THE PLAYERS!

GOALKEEPERS	
Fabio Coltorti	Grasshoppers Zurich
Pascal Zuberbuehler	Basel
DEFENDERS	
Philipp Degen	Borussia Dortmund
Stephane Grichting	Auxerre
Stephane Henchoz	Wigan
Ludovic Magnin	Stuttgart
Patrick Mueller	Lyon
Philippe Senderos	Arsenal
Boris Smiljanic	Basel
Christoph Spycher	Eintracht Frankfurt
Murat Yakin	Basel
MIDFIELDERS	
Tranquillo Barnetta	Bayer Leverkusen
Valon Behrami	Lazio
Ricardo Cabanas	FC Koln
Daniel Gygax	Lille
Benjamin Huggel	Eintracht Frankfurt
Johann Lonfat	Sochaux
Johann Vogel	AC Milan
Raphael Wicky	Hamburg
Hakan Yakin	Young Boys
Reto Ziegler	Tottenham
STRIKERS	
Alexander Frei	Rennes
Mauro Lustrinelli	Thun
Alexandre Rey	Neuchatel Xamax
Marco Streller	Cologne
Johan Vonlanthen	PSV

TEAMTALK!

Switzerland had to qualify through the play-offs, but don't let that fool you! They beat a difficult Turkey team and are now a much better side than the one England whupped at Euro 2004. Their young team is full of talent and star striker Johan Vonlanthen is Switzerland's answer to Wayne Rooney! Their main problems are that they haven't got loads of experience and aren't a very physical team either, which could be a big problem if they get to the knockout stages of the competition.

MATCHMAN'S VERDICT: "DA SWISS AIN'T GONNA ROLL OVER AT DA WORLD CUP, BUT I CAN'T SEE 'EM GOIN' MUCH FURTHER THAN DA SECOND ROUND!"

PLAYER TO WATCH!

Johan Vonlanthen

The striker was one of Switzerland's few plus points at Euro 2004, when he became the youngest ever scorer in the Euro Championship finals at just 18. He has serious pace and will be a real handful for defenders!

SOUTH KOREA!

| COACH! | DICK ADVOCAAT | WORLD RANKING! | 29TH | WORLD CUP ODDS! | 300/1 | WORLD CUP BEST! | SEMI-FINALS 2002 |

STRONGEST STARTING LINE-UP! 3-4-3

LEE WOON JAE

YOU KYOUNG YOUL — KIM JIN KYU — CHOI JIN CHEUL

PARK JI SUNG — SEOL KI HYEON — LEE EUL YONG — LEE YOUNG PYO

CHA DU RI — LEE DONG GOOK — AHN JUNG HWAN

ROAD TO THE FINALS!

Asia Group 1	P	W	D	L	F	A	Pts
Saudi Arabia	6	4	2	0	10	1	14
South Korea	6	3	1	2	9	5	10
Uzbekistan	6	1	2	3	7	11	5
Kuwait	6	1	1	4	4	13	4

RESULT	SCORE	OPPOSITION	H/A
Won	2-0	Kuwait	H
Lost	2-0	Saudi Arabia	A
Won	2-1	Uzbekistan	H
Drew	1-1	Uzbekistan	A
Won	0-4	Kuwait	A
Lost	0-1	Saudi Arabia	A

TOP SCORER	
Lee Dong Gook	5

Lee Dong Gook.

TEAMTALK!

South Korea struggled to even qualify for Germany 2006, despite reaching the 2002 World Cup semi-finals in sensational style. After losing two of their six games and finishing second in the group to Saudi Arabia, coach Jo Bonfrere was sacked and replaced by Dick Advocaat. The ex-Rangers boss has a young side with plenty of attacking options, but he hasn't had many games to work with the squad and they look dodgy at the back. South Korea will struggle, so don't expect heroics again!

MATCHMAN'S VERDICT: "THEM CRAZY SOUTH KOREANS WERE THE SHOCK OF THE 2002 WORLD CUP, BUT NOW I RECKS IT'S OUT IN DA FIRST ROUND!"

PLAYER TO WATCH!

Park Ji Sung
The Man. United midfielder ripped up the Premiership last season, and South Korea will be hoping their star man can produce more of the same! His wicked skills, tricks, hard work and goals will be vital in Group G!

TOGO!

| COACH! | OTTO PFISTER | WORLD RANKING! | 56TH | WORLD CUP ODDS! | 400/1 | WORLD CUP BEST! | DEBUT IN FINALS |

STRONGEST STARTING LINE-UP! 4-3-3

AGASSA

NIBOMBE — ABALO — DOSSEH — ATTE-OUDEY

CHERIF TOURE — AZIAWONOU — MAMAH

ADEBAYOR — COUBADJA TOURE — SENAYA

ROAD TO THE FINALS!

Africa Group 1	P	W	D	L	F	A	Pts
Togo	10	7	2	1	20	8	23
Senegal	10	6	3	1	21	8	21
Zambia	10	6	1	3	16	10	19
Congo	10	3	1	6	10	14	10
Mali	10	2	2	6	11	14	8
Liberia	10	1	1	8	3	27	4

RESULT	SCORE	OPPOSITION	H/A
Lost	1-0	Zambia	A
Won	3-1	Senegal	H
Drew	0-0	Liberia	A
Won	2-0	Congo	H
Won	1-0	Mali	H
Won	2-1	Mali	A
Won	4-1	Zambia	H
Drew	2-2	Senegal	A
Won	3-0	Liberia	H
Won	3-2	Congo	H

TOP SCORER	
Emmanuel Adebayor	11

Junior Yao Senaya.

TEAMTALK!

Togo were so chuffed to qualify for their first ever World Cup finals, they all took a day's national holiday to celebrate! With such a young team, not much is expected of them in the finals, though that could work in their favour. There's no doubt they've got some talented players, but they rely heavily on Emmanuel Adebayor for goals and often start slowly in games. If they start off on the back foot or teams shut off the supply to their No.1 striker, the tournament rookies may find it too difficult to cope.

MATCHMAN'S VERDICT: "TOGO TIP-TOPPED THEIR GROUP, BUT THEY IS GONNA FIND IT HARDER GOIN' NOW! I RECKS IT'S AN EARLY TRIP HOME - SOZ!"

PLAYER TO WATCH!

Emmanuel Adebayor
The young Arsenal striker was on fire in qualifying, scoring 11 goals – that's half Togo's total! At 6ft 3ins, he's great in the air but is also pacy, holds the ball up well, has lightning-quick feet and loves to get behind defenders.

MATCHMAN'S

WELCOME TO PART THREE OF ME WICKEDY WORLD CUP QUIZ! IT'S TIME TO SHOW WOT YA KNOW 'BOUT DA TEAMS!

BADGE IT!

WHICH COUNTRY'S BADGE 'AS BEEN GIVEN DA SPIN?

10 POINTS FOR CORRECT ANSWER

ANSWER

MY SCORE /10

TOP CAP!

WHICH OF THESE FRANCE GUYS 'AS WON DA MOST CAPS? GIVE DA DUDE WITH THE MOST 1 AND DA LEAST 5!

THIERRY HENRY — 1
LUDOVIC GIULY — 2
CLAUDE MAKELELE — 3
LILIAN THURAM — 4
MIKAEL SILVESTRE — 5

2 POINTS FOR EACH CORRECT ANSWER

MY SCORE /10

IN THE LIONS DEN!

CAN YA SPOT FIVE OF PORTUGAL'S BRAVE FOOTY STARS HIDIN' IN THIS SCARY SPAIN CROWD?

2 POINTS FOR EACH CORRECT ANSWER

MY SCORE /10

CLUB & COUNTRY!

MATCH THESE KICKIN' COUNTRIES WIV DA WICKED CLUBS WHAT PLAY THERE! IT'S WELL EASY!

 HOLLAND SEVILLA

 ARGENTINA BOCA JUNIORS

 SPAIN SAMPDORIA

 AUSTRALIA VITESSE ARNHEM

 ITALY ADELAIDE UNITED

2 POINTS FOR EACH CORRECT ANSWER

MY SCORE /10

WORDFIT!

CHECK OUT THESE WICKED WORLD CUP TEAMS! FIT 'EM ALL IN DA RIGHT SPACES FOR DA MAXIMUM TEN POINTS!

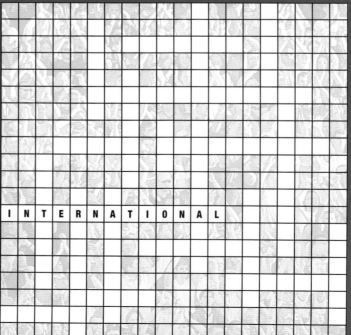

INTERNATIONAL

>> ARGENTINA
>> AUSTRALIA
>> BRAZIL
>> CZECH REPUBLIC
>> ENGLAND
>> FRANCE
>> GERMANY
>> GHANA
>> HOLLAND
>> ITALY
>> INTERNATIONAL
>> IVORY COAST
>> MEXICO
>> PARAGUAY
>> PORTUGAL
>> SOUTH KOREA
>> SPAIN
>> SWEDEN
>> TUNISIA
>> UKRAINE
>> USA

½ POINT FOR EACH CORRECT ANSWER

MY SCORE /10

QUIZ!

MANAGER MATCH-UP!

MATCH THESE GAFFERS WIV DA PLAYERS THEY WILL BE BOSSIN' ABOUT THIS SUMMER!

2 POINTS FOR EACH CORRECT ANSWER

MY SCORE /10

1 JURGEN KLINSMANN	2 SVEN GORAN ERIKSSON	3 ZICO	4 GUUS HIDDINK	5 MARCO VAN BASTEN

A RUUD VAN NISTELROOY	B BASTIAN SCHWEINSTEIGER	C PAUL ROBINSON	D HIDETOSHI NAKATA	E MARCO BRESCIANO

NATIONAL DRESS!

CAN YA SUSS OUT WHICH BRITISH BASED STAR IS HIDIN' OUT IN THE CLOTHES OF HIS HOME COUNTRY?

ANSWER

10 POINTS FOR CORRECT ANSWER

MY SCORE /10

BRAZIL QUIZ!

HOW MUCH DO YA KNOW 'BOUT DA MOST SUCCESSFUL TEAM IN WORLD CUP HISTORY? LET'S FIND OUT, DUDES!

1 Brazil will play in Group F with which European team?

ANSWER

2 Which country did Brazil lose to in the 1998 World Cup final?

ANSWER

3 What's the name of Arsenal's Brazilian midfield star?

ANSWER

4 True or False? Brazil have never missed a World Cup finals.

ANSWER

5 Where does Cafu play? Is it right-back or right-wing?

ANSWER

2 POINTS FOR EACH CORRECT ANSWER

MY SCORE /10

STRIKE BUDDIES!

FOLLOW DA LINE FROM DA WICKED GOAL GRABBER AT DA TOP DOWN TO DA CLUE, THEN LINK 'EM WIV THEIR STRIKE PARTNER! WHEN YOU'VE DONE THAT, WRITE THE COUNTRY THAT THEY BOTH PLAY FOR!

Our fans love wearing their crazy orange gear!	We are wicked strikers in Bundesliga footy!	We both scored for our country at Euro 2004!	We play for different club teams in Madrid!	This is our first big tournament together!

1 ANSWER	2 ANSWER	3 ANSWER	4 ANSWER	5 ANSWER

2 POINTS FOR EACH CORRECT ANSWER

MY SCORE /10

KITTED UP!

GERMANY WILL BE PACKED WIV COOL KITS, BUT CAN YA JOIN THESE TEAMS WITH DA RIGHT ONES?

2 POINTS FOR EACH CORRECT ANSWER

MY SCORE /10

1 CZECH REPUBLIC	2 ENGLAND	3 GHANA	4 ITALY	5 HOLLAND

A	B 14	C 11	D 3	E 19

ANSWERS!

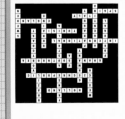

SPAIN!

COACH!	LUIS ARAGONES	CAPTAIN!	RAUL	MOST CAPS!	RAUL 92

QUALIFYING FORM!

Although they didn't lose a game, Spain's form wasn't good. They were expected to walk an easy group, but five poor draws meant they had to go through a play-off. They whupped Slovakia to book their place in the finals, but they'll have to do much better to taste World Cup glory!

STRENGTHS!

In almost every position, Spain have stars most other teams would love to be able to choose. From Casillas and Reina in goal, to Puyol and Marchena at the back, Joaquin and Xavi in midfield and Raul, Torres and Villa up front, the team is pure quality!

WEAKNESSES!

The same old story is told before every major tournament, but it's true that Spain do flop badly on the big stage. They reached the quarter-finals of World Cup 2002, but they should have done much better and that was the furthest they'd gone for years!

Asier del Horno.

CAN THEY WIN?

They've got enough quality to give it a really good go, but there are still questions about how they perform on the big stage. If they can finally get over those worries they could go a long way – possibly even reach the final! Major stars like Raul, Puyol, Xavi, Morientes and Alonso have won loads in their club careers, so now they want international success!

MATCHMAN'S VERDICT: "I LOVE HOLIDAYS IN SPAIN, AND DA TEAM AIN'T DAT BAD EITHER! NOT SURE IF DIS LOT 'AVE GOT WHAT IT TAKES!"

RESULTS AND LINE-UPS IN QUALIFYING!

BOSNIA-HERZ.	BELGIUM	LITHUANIA	SAN MARINO	SERBIA-MONT.	LITHUANIA	BOSNIA-HERZ.	SERBIA-MONT.
Drew 1-1 (a)	Won 2-0 (h)	Drew 0-0 (a)	Won 5-0 (h)	Drew 0-0 (a)	Won 1-0 (h)	Drew 1-1 (h)	Drew 1-1 (a)
Casillas	Casillas	Casillas	Casillas	Casillas	Casillas	Casillas	Casillas
Salgado	Salgado	Salgado	Salgado	Pablo Ibanez	Salgado	Salgado	Salgado
Romero	Del Horno	Capdevila	Del Horno 1	Del Horno	Del Horno	Lopez	Del Horno
Helguera	Marchena	Marchena	Marchena	Ramos	Marchena	Marchena 1	Marchena
Puyol	Puyol	Puyol	Puyol	Puyol	Puyol	Puyol	Puyol
Victor	Joaquin	Victor	Joaquin 1	Joaquin	Joaquin	Joaquin	Joaquin
Albelda	Albelda	Albelda	Xavi	Albelda	Albelda	Albelda	Xabi Alonso
Baraja	Xavi	Baraja	De La Pena	De La Pena	Xavi	Xavi	Xavi
Vicente 1	Reyes	Xavi	Luque	Xavi	Vicente	Vicente	Vicente
Raul	Raul 1	Luque	Raul 1	Reyes	Raul	Raul	Raul 1
Reyes	Torres	Raul	Torres 1	Torres	Torres	Torres	Torres
Substitutes:	**Substitutes:**	**Substitutes:**	**Substitutes:**	**Substitutes:**	**Substitutes:**	**Substitutes:**	**Substitutes:**
Morientes 50	Luque 1 53	Tamudo 53	Guti 1 46	Juanito 46	Luque 1 57	Juanito 8	Tamudo
Valeron 58	Xabi Alonso 58	Reyes 65	Villa 46	Raul 46	Luis Garcia 60	Luque 35	Luis Garcia
Xabi Alonso 70	Baraja 75	Torres 79	Guayre 71	Antonio Lopez 62	Sergio Ramos 74	Xabi Alonso 62	Luque

MOST GOALS!	RAUL 42	WORLD RANKING!	6TH	WORLD CUP ODDS!	12/1	WORLD CUP BEST!	SEMI-FINALS 1950

★ PLAYER TO WATCH! ★

Joaquin

If you want a lesson in wicked wing play, just watch Joaquin in action! The Real Betis ace is a classic wide man, bursting past defenders with a turn of pace or skipping around them with his quick feet and tricks!

★ STRONGEST STARTING LINE-UP! 4-4-2

CASILLAS

SALGADO · PUYOL · MARCHENA · DEL HORNO

JOAQUIN · ALBELDA · ALONSO · VICENTE

RAUL · TORRES

★ PLAYER TO WATCH! ★

Xabi Alonso

Liverpool's fine playmaker will be playing in his first World Cup, and his slick passing is key to Spain's rapid attacks. Alonso never looks rushed on the ball and he can score goals from distance too!

★ ROAD TO THE FINALS! ★

Group 7 Europe	P	W	D	L	F	A	Pts
Serbia-Montenegro	10	6	4	0	16	1	22
Spain	10	5	5	0	19	3	20
Bosnia-Herzegovina	10	4	4	2	12	9	16
Belgium	10	3	3	4	16	11	12
Lithuania	10	2	4	4	8	9	10
San Marino	10	0	0	10	2	40	0

TOP SCORERS	
Fernando Torres	7
Luis Garcia	3
Raul	3

Luis Garcia.

★ THE PLAYERS! ★

GOALKEEPERS	
Iker Casillas	Real Madrid
Pepe Reina	Liverpool
Victor Valdes	Barcelona

DEFENDERS	
Joan Capdevila	Deportivo
Asier del Horno	Chelsea
Pablo Ibanez	Atletico Madrid
Juanito	Real Betis
Antonio Lopez	Atletico Madrid
Carlos Marchena	Valencia
Carlos Puyol	Barcelona
Sergio Ramos	Real Madrid
Michel Salgado	Real Madrid

MIDFIELDERS	
David Albelda	Valencia
Xabi Alonso	Liverpool
Ruben Baraja	Valencia
Luis Garcia	Liverpool
Guti	Real Madrid
Joaquin	Real Betis
Ivan de La Pena	Espanyol
Vicente	Valencia
Xavi	Barcelona

STRIKERS	
Albert Luque	Newcastle
Fernando Morientes	Liverpool
Raul	Real Madrid
Jose Reyes	Arsenal
Fernando Torres	Atletico Madrid
David Villa	Valencia

Jose Reyes.

BELGIUM	SAN MARINO	SLOVAKIA	SLOVAKIA
Won 2-0 (a)	Won 6-0 (a)	Won 5-1 (h)	Drew 1-1 (a)
...sillas	Casillas	Casillas	Casillas
...gado	Pablo Ibanez	Salgado	Salgado
...ez	Lopez 1	Del Horno	Lopez
...rchena	Juanito	Pablo Ibanez	Pablo Ibanez
...ol	Ramos 2	Puyol	Puyol
...quin	De La Pena	Luis Garcia 3	Baraja
...elda	Albelda	Albelda	Xavi
...	Raul	Xavi	Xabi Alonso
...nte	Reyes	Reyes	Vicente
...l	Villa	Raul	Raul
...es 2	Torres 3	Torres 1	Torres
...bstitutes:	Substitutes:	SUBSTITUTES:	Substitutes:
...es 55	Baraja 58	Vicente 55	Villa 1 61
... 55	Vicente 68	Xabi Alonso 65	Morientes 65
...aja 70	Mista 72	Morientes 1 76	Sergio Ramos 74

Raul.

UKRAINE!

COACH!	OLEG BLOKHIN	WORLD RANKING!	40th	WORLD CUP ODDS!	50/1	WORLD CUP BEST! DEBUT IN FINALS

Andriy Shevchenko.

ROAD TO THE FINALS!

Group 2 Europe	P	W	D	L	F	A	Pts
Ukraine	12	7	4	1	18	7	25
Turkey	12	6	5	1	23	9	23
Denmark	12	6	4	2	24	12	22
Greece	12	6	3	3	15	9	21
Albania	12	4	1	7	11	20	13
Georgia	12	2	4	6	14	25	10
Kazakhstan	12	0	1	11	6	29	1

RESULT	SCORE	OPPOSITION	H/A
Drew	1-1	Denmark	A
Won	2-1	Kazakhstan	A
Drew	1-1	Greece	H
Won	2-0	Georgia	H
Won	3-0	Turkey	A
Won	2-0	Albania	A
Won	1-0	Denmark	H
Won	2-0	Kazakhstan	H
Won	1-0	Greece	H
Drew	1-1	Georgia	A
Lost	1-0	Turkey	H
Drew	2-2	Albania	H

TOP SCORER

Andriy Shevchenko	6

Andrey Voronin.

THE PLAYERS!

GOALKEEPERS

Vitaly Reva	Dynamo Kiev
Alexandr Shovkoskiy	Dynamo Kiev

DEFENDERS

Vyacheslav Chicher	Mariupol
Sergeiy Fedorov	Dynamo Kiev
Sergey Matiukhin	Dnipropetrovsk
Andriy Nesmachny	Dynamo Kiev
Aleksandr Radchenko	Dnipropetrovsk
Andrey Rusol	Dnipropetrovsk
Mikhail Starostyak	Yaroslavl
Anatoliy Tymoshyuk	Shakhtar Donetsk
Vladimir Yezerski	Dnipropetrovsk
Sergiy Zadorozhny	Dnipropetrovsk

MIDFIELDERS

Ruslan Bidnenko	Dnipropetrovsk
Oleg Gusev	Dynamo Kiev
Andriy Husin	Dynamo Kiev
Sergei Nazarenko	Dnipropetrovsk
Ruslan Rotan	Dynamo Kiev
Oleg Shelaev	Dnipropetrovsk
Anataly Timoshchuk	Shakhtar Donetsk
Sergiy Zakarlyuka	Metalurh Donetsk

STRIKERS

Alexei Belik	Shakhtar Donetsk
Sergei Rebrov	Dynamo Kiev
Andriy Shevchenko	AC Milan
Andriy Vorobey	Shakhtar Donetsk
Andrey Voronin	Bayer Leverkusen

STRONGEST STARTING LINE-UP! 4-3-3

SHOVKOSKIY

YEZERSKI — TYMOSHYUK — RUSOL — NESMACHNY

GUSEV — HUSIN — ROTAN

VOROBEY — SHEVCHENKO — VORONIN

TEAMTALK!

Ukraine became the first European team to qualify for Germany 2006, and then went on to top a tricky group that had Turkey, Denmark and European champs Greece fighting it out. It's their first appearance at the World Cup finals so they'll be looking to impress, and their forward line, led by AC Milan ace Andriy Shevchenko, looks very tasty. But their midfield isn't strong and has no star names, and this could count against them. If Sheva doesn't fire, Ukraine's chances don't look too promising!

MATCHMAN'S VERDICT: "WIV SHEVA IN DA SIDE, THEY COULD GET OUT OF THE GROUP BUT NOT MUCH FURTHER. LATERS!"

PLAYER TO WATCH!

Andriy Vorobey

It would be a big mistake for teams to concentrate just on Shevchenko – his strike partner Vorobey is a threat too. Once a Ukrainian Golden Boot winner, Vorobey has bags of experience and is a lively forward who can play deeper!

Oleg Gusev.

TUNISIA!

COACH!	ROGER LEMERRE	WORLD RANKING!	28TH	WORLD CUP ODDS!	300/1	WORLD CUP BEST!	FIRST ROUND 1978, 1998, 2002

★ STRONGEST STARTING LINE-UP! 4-4-2 ★

BOUMNIJEL

TRABELSI — CLAYTON — JAIDI — HAGUI

BENACHOUR — BOUAZIZI — CHADI — MNARI

JAZIRI — DOS SANTOS

★ ROAD TO THE FINALS! ★

Group 5 Africa	P	W	D	L	F	A	Pts
Tunisia	10	6	3	1	25	9	21
Morocco	10	5	5	0	17	7	20
Guinea	10	5	2	3	15	10	17
Kenya	10	3	1	6	8	17	10
Botswana	10	3	0	7	10	18	9
Malawi	10	1	3	6	12	26	6

RESULT	SCORE	OPPOSITION	H/A
Won	4-1	Botswana	H
Lost	1-2	Guinea	A
Drew	1-1	Morocco	A
Drew	2-2	Malawi	A
Won	7-0	Malawi	H
Won	3-1	Botswana	A
Won	2-0	Guinea	H
Won	1-0	Kenya	H
Won	2-0	Kenya	A
Drew	2-2	Morocco	H

TOP SCORER	
Francileudo Dos Santos	6

Jose Clayton.

★ TEAMTALK! ★

Tunisia have been to three World Cup finals and never got past the group stages – but this summer could be their best chance yet! They needed a late equalizer against Morocco to book their place at Germany 2006, but under coach Roger Lemerre the team have improved loads and are a hard-to-beat unit. The former France coach will be confident of his team reaching the knockout stages, but it could boil down to how much they believe in themselves. This group gives them a golden opportunity!

 MATCHMAN'S VERDICT: "TUNISIA AIN'T A MEGA NAME IN WORLD FOOTBALL, BUT THEY COULD BE FIGHTIN' IT OUT WIV DA UKRAINE FOR SECOND SPOT IN GROUP H!"

★ PLAYER TO WATCH! ★

Francileudo Dos Santos
This striker could have played for Brazil – and we know why! The little man moves well and is lightning-quick with the ball at his feet. He bagged six strikes in qualifying – including four in one game – and will be going for goals!

SAUDI ARABIA!

COACH!	GABRIEL CALDERON	WORLD RANKING!	32ND	WORLD CUP ODDS!	750/1	WORLD CUP BEST!	SECOND ROUND 1994

★ STRONGEST STARTING LINE-UP! 4-4-2 ★

ZAID

AL BAHRI — AL HALWI — AL MONTASHARI — FALLATHA

KHARIRI — AL DOSSARI — AL SHLHOUB — TEMYAT

AL JABER — AL KHATANI

★ ROAD TO THE FINALS! ★

Stage 2 Group 8	P	W	D	L	F	A	Pts
Saudi Arabia	6	6	0	0	14	1	18
Turkmenistan	6	2	1	3	8	10	7
Indonesia	6	2	1	3	8	12	7
Sri Lanka	6	0	2	4	4	11	2

Stage 3 Group A	P	W	D	L	F	A	Pts
Saudi Arabia	6	4	2	0	10	1	14
South Korea	6	3	1	2	9	5	10
Uzbekistan	6	1	2	3	7	11	5
Kuwait	6	1	1	4	4	13	4

RESULT	SCORE	OPPOSITION	H/A
Won	3-0	Indonesia	H
Won	1-0	Sri Lanka	A
Won	3-0	Turkmenistan	H
Won	1-0	Turkmenistan	A
Won	3-1	Indonesia	A
Won	3-0	Sri Lanka	H
Drew	1-1	Uzbekistan	A
Won	2-0	South Korea	H
Drew	0-0	Kuwait	A
Won	3-0	Kuwait	H
Won	3-0	Uzbekistan	H
Won	1-0	Saudi Arabia	A

TOP SCORERS	
Ibrahim Al Shahrani	3
Mohammad Al Shlhoub	3
Sami Al Jaber	3

Redha Fallatha.

★ TEAMTALK! ★

Saudi Arabia were pants at the last World Cup, and it looks like they might not be much better this time around! They lost all three games in South Korea & Japan, and were whupped 8-0 by Germany. But they have got a mean defence now and only let in one goal in each of their qualifying groups, so if they can keep things tight at the back, they could sneak the odd goal through Saudi legend Sami Al Jaber. Their clash against Tunisia will be a big one in the fight to reach the second round!

 **MATCHMAN'S VERDICT:** "DA SAUDIS COULD BECOME DA WHIPPIN' BOYS OF DIS WC GROUP IF THEY AIN'T CAREFUL. OUCHEE!"

★ PLAYER TO WATCH! ★

Sami Al Jaber
This will be the 34-year-old superstar's fourth and final World Cup – and he'll want to go out with a bang! Al Jaber's been playing for Saudi Arabia for 17 years and he came out of retirement to lead his country to Germany 2006!

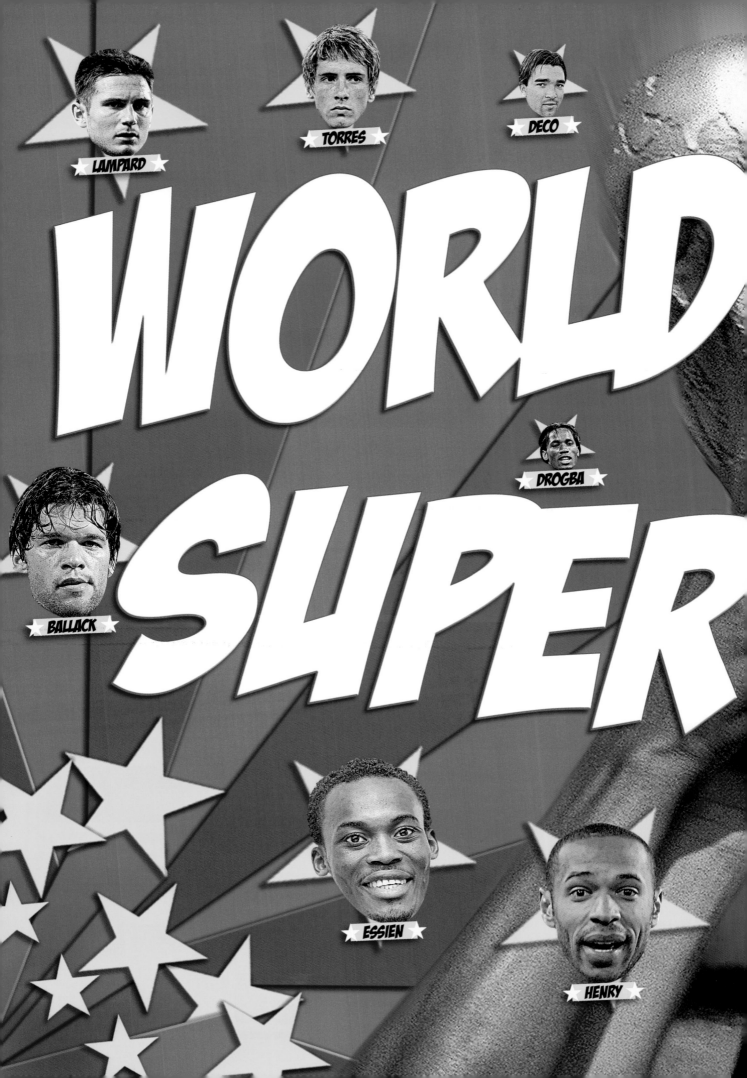

KAKA

ROONEY

RONALDINHO

CUP STARS!

SHEVCHENKO

VAN DER VAART

Who's gonna rock the World Cup?
MATCH picks 20 stars to watch!

RONALDO

VAN NISTELROOY

CASILLAS

MICHAEL BALLACK

GERMANY

AGE: 29
POSITION: MIDFIELDER

Ballack will be Germany's key player – he's so important that the hosts have even been called a one-man team! The ace midfielder will be hoping to go one better than the 2002 World Cup, when he scored in the quarter-final and semi-final, but was suspended as Germany lost to Brazil in the final!

IKER CASILLAS

SPAIN

AGE: 25
POSITION: GOALKEEPER

Casillas already has one World Cup campaign under his belt. In 2002 he jumped into the No.1 spot when Santiago Canizares was injured before the tournament and played in all of Spain's games. The Real Madrid star saved three penalties in the tournament and has been first choice ever since!

DECO

PORTUGAL

AGE: 28
POSITION: MIDFIELDER

Born in Brazil but qualified to play for Portugal, Deco showed his new fans what a magical player he is to help his team reach the Euro 2004 final! Now he's taken over from legend Luis Figo as Portugal's midfield ace and, after ripping it up for Barcelona, he could be one of the World Cup's big stars!

DIDIER DROGBA

IVORY COAST

AGE: 28

POSITION: STRIKER

Watch out for Drogba – he's gonna be up for the World Cup! With nine goals in qualifying, he was the Ivory Coast's leading scorer and the Chelsea striker is their big hope this summer! Italy boss Marcello Lippi called Drogba 'outstanding' when the teams drew 1-1 in a friendly last November!

MICHAEL ESSIEN

GHANA

AGE: 23
POSITION: MIDFIELDER

Ghana are in a difficult group at their first World Cup finals – but at least they have a player who can mix it with the best! Essien made his name at French side Lyon, before a £24 million move to Chelsea in 2005 made him one of the world's most expensive players. Ghana won't be easy to beat with him around!

THIERRY HENRY

FRANCE

AGE: 28
POSITION: STRIKER

Henry's out for revenge – coz
the 2002 World Cup was a disaster!
He was sent off, he didn't score and
France crashed out in the group stages!
As one of the world's best strikers,
Arsenal ace Henry has the goalscoring
skills to make sure the 1998 winners
do a lot better this time around!

★ ZLATAN ★
★ IBRAHIMOVIC ★
SWEDEN
AGE: 24
POSITION: STRIKER

The last two seasons have seen Ibrahimovic go from strength to strength! A tall striker with expert control and clinical finishing, the Swede showed his class at Euro 2004 with an amazing backheeled volley goal against Italy! Expect to see even more of his awesome skills in Germany!

★ KAKA ★
BRAZIL
AGE: 24
POSITION: MIDFIELDER

Brazil's squad is packed with attacking talent, but coach Carlos Alberto Parreira has Kaka down on the teamsheet as a definite starter! The AC Milan star likes to play just behind the strikers, where he can get into dangerous positions and play the killer pass. He's a deadly finisher too!

FRANK LAMPARD

ENGLAND

AGE: 27
POSITION: MIDFIELDER

Lampard has been amazing for England and Chelsea for the last few seasons! He hardly ever misses a game, he's super-fit, an excellent passer and, best of all, scores plenty of goals! Most of his shots are on target and he's a free-kick and penalty king too! Lamps is gonna rock in Germany!

LIONEL MESSI

ARGENTINA

AGE: 18
POSITION: MIDFIELDER

Messi turns 19 during the World Cup and could celebrate his birthday by becoming a real superstar! After scoring six goals in seven games to help Argentina win the Under-20 World Championship in 2005, and breaking into Barcelona's star-studded line-up, all eyes will be on the top teenager!

JUAN ROMAN RIQUELME

ARGENTINA

AGE: 27
POSITION: MIDFIELDER

Riquelme is the comeback king! The classy midfielder wasn't a success at Barcelona, but a move to Villarreal changed everything and now he's one of the most creative players in the world! He's not quick, but he's a superb playmaker who controls games and punishes the opposition!

ROBINHO
BRAZIL
AGE: 22
POSITION: STRIKER

This Brazil sensation will be battling against Adriano and Ronaldo for a place in the starting line-up. But if he gets a chance to show off his skills, Robinho will not disappoint! The Real Madrid star loves to attack from wide positions and is a dribbling wizard – watch his super-quick feet tie defenders in knots!

RONALDINHO

BRAZIL

AGE: 26
POSITION: MIDFIELDER

At the 2002 World Cup, Ronaldinho showed flashes of his brilliance – but this summer he enters the tournament as the best player on the planet! Ronnie can beat defenders, make goals, score from all angles and win games on his own. Brazil will be the team to beat, and Ronaldinho will be their star!

CRISTIANO RONALDO

PORTUGAL

AGE: 21

POSITION: MIDFIELDER

There aren't many players who are more exciting to watch than Ronaldo! When he's in top form, the winger can dribble past three or four players, whip in a cracking cross or take a shot at goal himself! The Man. United star is good with his head as well, so he's a threat from free-kicks and corners!

WAYNE ROONEY

ENGLAND

AGE: 20
POSITION: STRIKER

After banging in the goals at Euro 2004, the whole world knows what Rooney can do – but stopping him is tough! He didn't score during the qualifying matches, but don't be fooled by that – the striker will still be England's most dangerous attacking player in the World Cup! Rooney can rock the tournament!

ANDRIY SHEVCHENKO

UKRAINE

AGE: 29
POSITION: STRIKER

Sheva has been one of the world's best strikers for years, but amazingly he's never played at a World Cup finals! The AC Milan hitman is desperate to make up for lost time and will be out to claim the Golden Boot top scorer prize. Watch out Spain, Tunisia and Saudi Arabia, coz Super Sheva is ready to rule!

FERNANDO TORRES

SPAIN

AGE: 22
POSITION: STRIKER

Fernando Torres is Spain's wonderkid and, with six goals in five World Cup qualifying games, it's easy to see why so much is expected of him! Blessed with power, pace and deadly finishing, the Atletico Madrid striker makes up a devastating attack along with Raul, Jose Reyes and Joaquin!

FRANCESCO TOTTI

ITALY

AGE: 29

POSITION: MIDFIELDER

Totti is one of the most gifted Italian players of the last ten years, and this could be his last chance to make his mark on a major tournament! He was a big letdown at Euro 2004 when he was banned for spitting, but on his day the Roma captain can score wonderful goals and create loads of chances!

RAFAEL VAN DER VAART

HOLLAND

AGE: 23
POSITION: MIDFIELDER

Van der Vaart's surprise move from Ajax to Hamburg in 2005 worked wonders for the Dutch midfielder! He has rediscovered his best form and slammed in the goals with the Bundesliga side. Dutch coach Marco van Basten knows he can be a key player for the team!

★ RUUD
VAN NISTELROOY ★
HOLLAND
AGE: 29
POSITION: STRIKER

Van Nistelrooy had to watch the last World Cup on TV, after Holland failed to qualify for the tournament. This time around, the master goalscorer will lead the forward line of a Dutch side that is definitely one of the faves to lift the trophy! You can expect Ruud to hit a hatful of goals in Germany!

THE WORLD CUP

61

62
Amazing! You head a last-minute winner against Germany in the semi-final! Bring on Brazil!
Take an extra turn

63

64

65

60

59
You pick up a booking for taking your shirt off to celebrate! Best not get any more of them!
Go back to square 42

58

57
You smash in a 30-yard equaliser in the quarter-finals! It sets the team on track to another win!
Move to square 65

56
England cruise to the knockout stage, and you're named Man Of The Match as the team win again!
Take an extra turn

41
The injured striker tells the papers he can't stand you stealing his headlines! That's not good!
Go back to square 22

42

43

44
Ouch! You bust a bone in your ankle and could be out for a while. Will you be fit enough to go to the World Cup?
Go back to square 24

45

40

39

38
A first-choice striker gets injured, so you're thrown straight into the team for your England debut!
Move to square 58

37

36

21
Aarrrgghh! Your debut goal is ruled out for offside! And your confidence takes a knock!
Miss a turn

22

23

24

25
You've been playing so well that papers start a campaign to get you picked for England! Awesome!
Move to square 35

20

19

18
What a start! You slam in a goal on your debut for your new team and the fans go crazy!
Move to square 39

17

16

START
Roll both dice to kick-off! Good luck, dudes!

2

3
You've been banging the goals in for your club in the lower divisions, and you end the season as top scorer! *Move to square 17*

4

5
Your wicked form has attracted loads of attention from Premiership clubs! You keep your fingers crossed for a big move! *Take an extra turn*

HERO GAME!

'AVE YOU GOT WOT IT TAKES TO GET SPOTTED BY SVEN AND LEAD ENGLAND TO WORLD CUP GLORY? GRAB TWO DICE AND A LOAD OF MATES AND FIND OUT!

66 these games have really taken it out of you – you're shattered!
Go back to square 54

67

68

HOO-OOFF!

69 Nooooo! You balloon a penalty over the bar in the World Cup final! How embarrassing!
Go back to square 51

70 Get in! A hat-trick in the final brings the World Cup back to England. You're the hero!

55

54

53 You get roughed up by some tough defenders and struggle for a few days. Get some rest!
Go back to square 33

52 You get on the scoresheet in the opening game, then go on to hit three more goals in the group stages! Move to square 68

51

46

47 You recover from injury and make the cut for the squad! You're going to Germany!
Move to square 55

48

49

50

35

34 The media campaign works – Sven finally calls you up! Now's your big chance to shine!
Take an extra turn

33

32

31

26

27

28

29

30 One of the tabloids reckons you're just lucky, and tells Sven not to give you a go! Harsh!
Go back to square 10

15

14 No way! The deal gets put on hold coz your agent says he wants more dosh! Eh?
Go back to square 7

13 Great news! A top Prem club has made a mega offer, and your gaffer has accepted. You're off to the big time!
Move to square 28

12

11

6

7

8

9 The rest of the lads get jealous of you, and say they're not gonna pass to you any more! Gutted!
Go back to square 6

10

GROUP A | GERMANY ★ COSTA RICA ★ POLAND ★ ECUADOR

GERMANY v COSTA RICA	ECUADOR v COSTA RICA
June 9, 5.00pm in Munich	June 15, 2.00pm in Hamburg
POLAND v ECUADOR	ECUADOR v GERMANY
June 9, 8.00pm in Gelsenkirchen	June 20, 3.00pm in Berlin
GERMANY v POLAND	COSTA RICA v POLAND
June 14, 8.00pm in Dortmund	June 20, 3.00pm in Hanover

GROUP B | ENGLAND ★ PARAGUAY ★ TRINIDAD & TOBAGO ★ SWEDEN

ENGLAND v PARAGUAY	SWEDEN v PARAGUAY
June 10, 2.00pm in Frankfurt	June 15, 8.00pm in Berlin
TRINIDAD & TOBAGO v SWEDEN	PARAGUAY v TRINIDAD & TOBAGO
June 10, 5.00pm in Dortmund	June 20, 8.00pm in Kaiserslautern
ENGLAND v TRINIDAD & TOBAGO	SWEDEN v ENGLAND
June 15, 5.00pm in Nuremberg	June 20, 8.00pm in Cologne

GROUP C | ARGENTINA ★ IVORY COAST ★ SERBIA-MONTENEGRO ★ HOLLAND

ARGENTINA v IVORY COAST	HOLLAND v IVORY COAST
June 10, 8.00pm in Hamburg	June 16, 5.00pm in Stuttgart
SERBIA-MONTENEGRO v HOLLAND	HOLLAND v ARGENTINA
June 11, 2.00pm in Leipzig	June 21, 8.00pm in Frankfurt
ARGENTINA v SERBIA-MONTENEGRO	IVORY COAST v SERBIA-MONTENEGRO
June 16, 2.00pm in Gelsenkirchen	June 21, 8.00pm in Munich

GROUP D | MEXICO ★ IRAN ★ ANGOLA ★ PORTUGAL

MEXICO v IRAN	PORTUGAL v IRAN
June 11, 5.00pm in Nuremberg	June 17, 2.00pm in Frankfurt
ANGOLA v PORTUGAL	IRAN v ANGOLA
June 11, 8.00pm in Cologne	June 21, 3.00pm in Leipzig
MEXICO v ANGOLA	PORTUGAL v MEXICO
June 16, 8.00pm in Hanover	June 21, 3.00pm in Gelsenkirchen

WORLD CUP FIXT

SECOND ROUND!

SECOND ROUND ONE — June 24, 4.00pm in Munich

GROUP A WINNERS
GROUP B RUNNERS-UP

SECOND ROUND TWO — June 24, 8.00pm in Leipzig

GROUP C WINNERS
GROUP D RUNNERS-UP

SECOND ROUND THREE — June 25, 4.00pm in Stuttgart

GROUP B WINNERS
GROUP A RUNNERS-UP

SECOND ROUND FOUR — June 25, 8.00pm in Nuremberg

GROUP D WINNERS
GROUP C RUNNERS-UP

SECOND ROUND FIVE — June 26, 4.00pm in Kaiserslautern

GROUP E WINNERS
GROUP F RUNNERS-UP

SECOND ROUND SIX — June 26, 8.00pm in Cologne

GROUP G WINNERS
GROUP H RUNNERS-UP

SECOND ROUND SEVEN — June 27, 4.00pm in Dortmund

GROUP F WINNERS
GROUP E RUNNERS-UP

SECOND ROUND EIGHT — June 27, 8.00pm in Hanover

GROUP H WINNERS
GROUP G RUNNERS-UP

GROUP E ITALY ★ GHANA ★ USA ★ CZECH REPUBLIC

USA v CZECH REPUBLIC		ITALY v USA	
June 12, 5.00pm in Gelsenkirchen		June 16, 8.00pm in Kaiserslautern	

ITALY v GHANA		CZECH REPUBLIC v ITALY	
June 12, 8.00pm in Hanover		June 22, 3.00pm in Hamburg	

CZECH REPUBLIC v GHANA		GHANA v USA	
June 16, 5.00pm in Cologne		June 22, 3.00pm in Nuremberg	

GROUP G FRANCE ★ SWITZERLAND ★ SOUTH KOREA ★ TOGO

SOUTH KOREA v TOGO		TOGO v SWITZERLAND	
June 13, 2.00pm in Frankfurt		June 19, 2.00pm in Dortmund	

FRANCE v SWITZERLAND		TOGO v FRANCE	
June 13, 5.00pm in Stuttgart		June 23, 8.00pm in Cologne	

FRANCE v SOUTH KOREA		SWITZERLAND v SOUTH KOREA	
June 18, 8.00pm in Leipzig		June 23, 8.00pm in Hanover	

GROUP F BRAZIL ★ CROATIA ★ AUSTRALIA ★ JAPAN

AUSTRALIA v JAPAN		BRAZIL v AUSTRALIA	
June 12, 2.00pm in Kaiserslautern		June 18, 5.00pm in Munich	

BRAZIL v CROATIA		JAPAN v BRAZIL	
June 13, 8.00pm in Berlin		June 22, 8.00pm in Dortmund	

JAPAN v CROATIA		CROATIA v AUSTRALIA	
June 18, 2.00pm in Nuremberg		June 22, 8.00pm in Stuttgart	

GROUP H SPAIN ★ UKRAINE ★ TUNISIA ★ SAUDI ARABIA

SPAIN v UKRAINE		SPAIN v TUNISIA	
June 14, 2.00pm in Leipzig		June 19, 8.00pm in Stuttgart	

TUNISIA v SAUDI ARABIA		UKRAINE v TUNISIA	
June 14, 5.00pm in Munich		June 23, 3.00pm in Berlin	

SAUDI ARABIA v UKRAINE		SAUDI ARABIA v SPAIN	
June 19, 5.00pm in Hamburg		June 23, 3.00pm in Kaiserslautern	

RES GUIDE!

Using your weekly copy of *MATCH*, fill in the results of each game, then write in the teams as they qualify – all the way up to the *WORLD CUP FINAL* on Sunday, July 9 in Berlin!

QUARTER-FINALS!

QUARTER-FINAL ONE	June 30, 4.00pm in Berlin
SECOND ROUND ONE WINNERS	
SECOND ROUND TWO WINNERS	

QUARTER-FINAL TWO	June 30, 8.00pm in Hamburg
SECOND ROUND FIVE WINNERS	
SECOND ROUND SIX WINNERS	

QUARTER-FINAL THREE	July 1, 4.00pm in Gelsenkirchen
SECOND ROUND THREE WINNERS	
SECOND ROUND FOUR WINNERS	

QUARTER-FINAL FOUR	July 1, 8.00pm in Frankfurt
SECOND ROUND SEVEN WINNERS	
SECOND ROUND EIGHT WINNERS	

SEMI-FINALS!

SEMI-FINAL ONE	July 4, 8.00pm in Dortmund
QUARTER-FINAL ONE WINNERS	
QUARTER-FINAL TWO WINNERS	

SEMI-FINAL TWO	July 5, 8.00pm in Munich
QUARTER-FINAL THREE WINNERS	
QUARTER-FINAL FOUR WINNERS	

THE 2006 WORLD CUP FINAL!

July 9, 7.00pm in Berlin
SEMI-FINAL ONE WINNERS
SEMI-FINAL TWO WINNERS